The Year After

KATY E. MARTIN

Copyright © 2018 Katy E. Martin
All rights reserved.
ISBN: *9781986567411*

DEDICATION

Dear Beau, this book is all about you baby boy. Thank you for being a part of me, for gifting me growth, fuel, and strength. You are loved, you are missed, and like all good things, you are wild and free.

Dear Bereaved Parents, to the brave and the broken. To the heavy-hearted Mama's who have a new love for the moon, for rainstorms and for great depth. To those who feel like they will never be whole again, whose fragments are barely recognizable. This book is for you. May we find beauty in our cracks. May we discover the courage in our hearts. May we put our pieces back together differently. May we create a whole new work of art.

CONTENTS

Acknowledgments   *i*

PART I   MAY 31st 2017

CHAPTER 1   No Heartbeat

CHAPTER 2   The Delivery

CHAPTER 3   The Next Morning

CHAPTER 4   *Guilt*

CHAPTER 5   The Ceremony

PART II   SUMMER

CHAPTER 6   Fight or Flight

CHAPTER 7   Fear & the Ultimate Gift

CHAPTER 8   Suffering

PART III   FALL

CHAPTER 9   A Parking Spot on Pegasus

CHAPTER 10   The Fragility of Life

CHAPTER 11   Beau Bears

PART IV   WINTER

CHAPTER 12   The Christmas Stocking

CHAPTER 13   The Medium

CHAPTER 14   Courage

CHAPTER 15   Attitude

CHAPTER 16   Your Road

PART V   SPRING

CHAPTER 17   The Art Show

CHAPTER 18   The Mountain

PART VI   SUMMER

CHAPTER 19   Mother's Day

CHAPTER 20   Beau's Birthday

CHAPTER 21   A Diagnosis

PART VII   ANGEL BABY STORIES

CHAPTER 22   Beckett's Story

CHAPTER 23   Kaiden's Story

CHAPTER 24   Marlowe's Story

CHAPTER 25   Braden's Story

CHAPTER 26   Daniel's Story

CHAPTER 27   Noah's Story

PART VIII   About the Author

ACKNOWLEDGMENTS

First, I need to thank Beau. My sweet boy, without you this book would not exist. My husband Brodie, you have been my biggest supporter, and have encouraged my writing from the very beginning. Thank you for your patience with me, and for your unwavering strength, and love. I also need to thank my friends, and family for their support throughout the year, specifically my mom Carmen, Brodie's mom Gini, my cousin Bronwen, and my two closest friends Alexa, and Haleigh. Thank you for continuing to check in, for always being thoughtful, and for showing me that I have a voice, and a story to share. I need to thank Amelia Barnes for not only being a guiding light, but a huge inspiration, as well as the ever growing tribe of women that I have had the honour to meet, and whom have offered their stories in this book as well. Lastly, I would like to thank my friends, and colleagues Neil Bridgeman, Joy Dell, and Courtney Chandler for taking on the painful task of editing.

"She made broken look beautiful and strong look invincible. She walked with the universe on her shoulders and made it look like a pair of wings."

- Ariana Dancu

PART I
May 31st 2017

CHAPTER 1
No Heartbeat

Four words.

There is no heartbeat.

    The morning of May 30, 2017, was like any other. My husband Brodie and I woke up smiling, looking at my eight and a half-month pregnant belly. We got ready for work, made some tea for the road, and began our short commute. I wasn't in any particular discomfort, and couldn't believe how well I had been feeling during most of this pregnancy. This was our first baby so all of our experiences were new, and I wasn't always sure what I should or shouldn't be feeling. I hadn't felt our baby have any strong kicks in what seemed like a day or so. So being the Millennial that I am, I went straight to the Google machine. I Googled, and Googled, and everything I read said baby moved less during the last few weeks as they start to run out of room.

    My husband and I are both teachers so he suggested that on our lunch break we go to the hospital and listen to the heartbeat just to reassure us. I remembered that I needed to get my blood drawn anyways, so thought it was a good idea. During my morning classes I spoke with a few of my colleagues about my concerns regarding the baby's movement. I was lovingly reassured that again, this is normal towards the end. I was convinced that I was probably overreacting. Regardless, Brodie met me at the hospital. I already had my blood work done by the time he got there, and so he had to convince me to go back into Emergency and listen to the heartbeat.

    The first nurse dealing with us could not find the heartbeat. She called in another nurse, who again searched but could not pick up the heartbeat on the doppler. At this point I still really did not think anything was wrong. How could it be? I was so healthy, my baby was so strong and big and every appointment went so well. All I kept telling myself was maybe I will be delivering our boy today.

We always celebrated when we hit certain milestones in the pregnancy and we had just recently celebrated because we knew our baby was strong enough to breathe and digest food on his own if I went into labor early. So again, it truly had not crossed my mind at this point that our baby could in fact be dead. In retrospect, I should have realized something was very wrong when the room started to fill with more medical staff. Two or three doctors came in and a few nurses were still in the room. A very tall and calm man, named Dr. Milligan entered with a mobile ultrasound machine. For some reason I couldn't look at the screen. The air seemed to be sucked out of the hospital room. Dr. Milligan, bit his lower lip and said, "There is no heartbeat." "I'm so sorry you guys." *There is no heartbeat...there is no heartbeat*, continued to echo over and over in my head. I remember Brodie grabbing me and pulling me into his arms, and the nurses rushing over and embracing us both. I can still hear my glasses hitting the hospital floor as they flew off my face. I can still feel the rawness from my full, and naive heart shattering into fragments that are, to this day, barely recognizable. I felt like I was in a daze. I still didn't quite understand. How could this have happened? I remember asking the Doctor, "How sure are you?" In the hopes that somehow these instruments could be wrong. He responded with, "99.5%, but just to be sure we will send you down to the ultrasound wing and get proper images." Tears streaming down our faces, we got in the elevator and found the ultrasound room where we were asked to go. The ultrasound technician happened to be a new friend of ours, and our heartbreak was echoed in her eyes. I lay on the table, holding Brodie's hand while the images were taken.

Brodie and I got back to our hospital room and stared out the window crying for hours. It's a kind of brokenness that makes your chest feel like it will cave in and the only thing stopping it are the gasps of air you take in between tears. It's a feeling of losing your breath and knowing you'll never be able to catch it again. Inside I felt so much to blame for whatever had happened to our sweet baby boy that I was scared to find out any information. Every time the thought about how this could somehow be my fault entered my mind, I pushed it out with everything I had. I somehow knew that I had to muster every ounce of strength within me to deliver our baby boy. This physical task was literally all I thought about. I couldn't think about our son Beau, or all that I had lost, or that it could somehow be my fault. It was all too hard. All I let myself think about was how to get through this delivery without harming my body anymore. All I kept saying to Brodie was that I wanted to fast forward through all of this.

I know now that I was in shock. I wanted to get through the delivery, recover for a few days at home, and go right back to work. I wanted to pretend this never happened to me, to us. How could this have happened? Wasn't karma a real thing? I've dedicated my life to being a kind and caring person. In fact, I've researched these things, and pushed myself as a human being to be better every day. I'm the person that actually does random acts of kindness, who makes thoughtful gifts, who prints out the recycling instructions in my community and posts it above our garbage cans. Clearly our beliefs regarding karma were now out the window. If this can happen, karma can't be real. It is interesting how tragedy and trauma really can reshape all that you thought you knew, or all that you thought you believed in. It has a way of poking holes in what you thought were concrete ideas.

While I lay in that hospital bed, in my hospital gown, unable to even touch my belly, all I felt emotionally was pain, a pain so deep and so vast that words truly fall short of its description. Yet, oddly, my brain was filled with such trivial things. I was in such a state of shock that I was worried about who would cover my class for the afternoon. I wanted to know exactly how much time I would need off to heal so that I could tell my Principals. In fact, my friend, and Vice Principal, Val, came in to see us and I remember telling her I would probably be back to work in about a week. The look on her face made me realize my response may not have been expected. Yet instead of making me feel like I just said something inappropriate she just hugged me. I thank her and many others for their understanding and kindness.

One of the nurses that I will never forget was named Alana. She is tall, blonde, very pretty, and carries herself with a graceful confidence. Alana brought us some reading material. Keep in mind, these booklets are made to help parents in our situation. In all honesty, they did provide us with some practical steps, and not to mention somewhere to focus our scattered attention. The problem with them lies in their titles. I kid you not, the first booklet Alana handed me was titled, *Empty Arms,* and the second was, *Shattered Dreams.* Really people, I think *Steps for Bereaved Parents,* would have sufficed. Nonetheless, I am oddly thankful for the distraction, and the dusty bit of humour we pulled from those covers.

The first person Brodie called was his Mom Gini. He left the room to make the call. He then called his brother Clint who came straight from work to see us in the hospital. Gini arrived after Clint and our dear friend Kathy came and stayed throughout the delivery as well. I am very close with my parents, but I was not able to reach them during this time. There are generally forty weeks in a pregnancy and what are the odds that the one-week my parents were on vacation would be the week that Beau would be born. My parents have always done a lot for my brother and I and we wanted to repay them in some way. So we planned a once in a lifetime trip for them to sail the Greek Islands for ten days. It was hard not being able to call my mom, but knowing they were having an incredible trip was something to focus on and smile about when everything else seemed so hard. I did get to call my brother who is a very logical and unemotional person, which was the best thing for me during those moments. I also got to call my closest friends, and my 96-year-old Nana asking for her prayers and strength.

Doctor Milligan explained our options to us. He explained that this was not an emergent situation and that if we wanted we could go home or to our regular hospital. Brodie and I both felt that we could not walk out of the hospital and that we wanted to deliver Beau as soon as possible. I feel some shame when I think about how I felt in those moments. I didn't feel motherly, I felt like I needed to get this baby out of me and I wanted to get as far away from the hospital as possible. Brodie and I both were not sure in the beginning if we wanted to see the baby, or how we could ever plan a funeral for him. I think this comes from an inner attempt to disassociate from such a difficult situation. I think there can be a deep fear in parents that if they hold their baby or name them or plan their funeral, it could make the whole situation that much harder. I am grateful that this train of thought didn't last long for us. I am also very thankful for the many nurses who encourage parents in these situations to hold their baby, to take pictures and to bond.

More than anything I was consumed by wanting to know how this happened. How did our perfect baby die? What did I do wrong? Early on, Dr. Milligan explained that in more than one third of stillborn cases parents don't get any answers. This didn't make sense to me. How could a baby die and no one know why? Dr. Milligan also said that once Beau was delivered we might get some clarity. He may find a visible blood clot, or notice infection in my amniotic fluid, or see a knot in the cord. I was terrified for any answer and also for no answer, but I knew regardless of the outcome we had to keep moving forward with the delivery.

CHAPTER 2
The Delivery

And so, I was induced. My labor hadn't started yet when the anesthesiologist came to see us. He was concerned about giving me an epidural so early, anticipating that it would in fact slow the whole process down. I think he was also confident that I would have a fairly quick labour, as Beau was thirty-four weeks and not yet full term. It was time for the anesthesiologist to go home and he did assure me that if I wanted him to come back at any time in the night he would. So we carried on without any freezing. We were at the hospital in Neepawa and if you know anything about that town you know the hospital is quite small as the population is no more than five-thousand. Thus, they had to page an on-call nurse to come in to help with the delivery through the night. Her name was Tara and she was perfect. With kindness in her eyes she almost single handedly got me through the hardest moment of my life. My labour started, and it was mild enough that I didn't really know it was labour. I remember the nurses asking me if I wanted a birthing ball or to walk around. I couldn't use any of the labor techniques I had read about only weeks before. I couldn't connect or associate those strategies with this situation, or perhaps I just didn't have the strength to leave that hospital bed. In the final stages of labour, I asked for some drugs to help me relax during contractions and my request was granted. Brodie was on my right side, steady and strong, and Tara was on my left coaching me through the entire thing. She had the skill and the courage to come face to face with me in those moments and I remember having enough sense to do exactly what she said. I remember only pushing three times and to everyone's surprise Beau came out on the third push, at 4:03am. *Lesson one that Beau has taught me:* I am so much stronger than I could have ever imagined. **"They name the most powerful storms after women for a reason."** – R.H. SIN

"They name the most powerful STORMS after women for a reason"

— r.h. Sin

I remember the room being so quiet except for the heartbroken sobs from the medical staff. I remember it being really dark in the delivery room, and my husband cutting the cord. I also remember seeing Dr. Milligan, and witnessing a stark contrast between this tall strong doctor and how he held my fragile baby boy with such tenderness and such care. I also remember Dr. Milligan taking an apologetic tone when he said that everything looked perfect…the cord…the placenta…the fluid, and our precious Beau. Of course HE was perfect. That is something I always knew.

I remember seeing Gini holding Beau, with tears streaming down her cheeks. She walked around the hospital room with him, bouncing her knees as if to soothe her sweet new grandson. To this day I often catch myself drifting off to those moments, witnessing my strong husband hold our boy whispering through his tears, "I'm sorry we couldn't protect you." I didn't realize it at the time, but looking back, Beau's delivery was short, and peaceful, and intimate, just like his life inside of me.

My heart could not be more thankful that we were in that hospital, with that staff, delivering Beau in the wee hours of the morning, when it felt like we were the only people in the world. It's like the whole world held its breath for just a moment, a precious moment, the only moment, and we got to spend it with our son.

As I held my perfect baby, a sense of calmness washed over me. Holding Beau was the first time my heart rate went back down, it was the first time I started breathing normally, and the first time I felt like I was back in my body. Brodie had the exact same experience. The whole process of losing a child is incredibly complex. The complexity in that moment came from the contrast between the joy and pride of looking at your beautiful baby boy and the indescribable heartache seeing them so still, knowing they will never take a breath, knowing you will never see them open their eyes, or laugh or cry or smile. I wanted so badly to be in that moment, and so badly to be out of that moment all at the same time. The nurses explained to us that we could take as long as we wanted and that they would take Beau whenever we needed and bring him back whenever we asked. I'm not exactly sure how long we got with Beau that night. To this day I struggle with wondering why I didn't ask to keep him the whole night, and wish that I would have spent more time with him, taken more pictures, and investigated his perfectly formed little body more. However, in those moments he seemed so fragile to me, and I didn't want to unwrap him or move him too much.

When a baby is born still most hospitals do not fill out a birth certificate. Graciously, Dr. Milligan filled out a certificate for us anyways, as a keepsake. He asked us how we spelt Beau and if he had a middle name. Beau always had a middle name. From early on in our pregnancy, even before we knew his first name, we knew we wanted him to wear Aemilius as his middle name after my Great Great Grandfather. The term emotional roller coaster was about to have a whole new meaning. I was about to witness the intricate flux of my emotions in the following moment. As we watched our little guy be measured and swaddled, we told Dr. Milligan his middle name was Aemilius. He then asked us if we could spell it. Brodie and I looked at each other and we both smiled because neither of us had any idea how it was spelt. Looking back now I think in that instance, the fact that we were able to see the humour in such a difficult moment was a foreshadowing...a telling that together we were going to be able to get through this great loss with grace, with hard work, and with love.

After Beau was all cleaned up the nurses brought him to me wrapped in a blanket, and Brodie and I had some time alone with our beautiful son.

CHAPTER 3
The Next Morning

We did get to see Beau the next morning and when we saw him he was in a beautiful, hand knitted, white bunting bag with velvety, white satin ribbon. It literally looked like the clothes of an angel. How fitting. A treasured memory to this day. These bunting bags are made by some wonderful women at the United Church in Minnedosa, our hometown, and donated to the hospital for angel babies like Beau.

Dr. Milligan brought us some paperwork to fill out. This was the first time I saw Brodie completely let down his guard and give into the all-encompassing grief. Seeing Beau's name, the name we spent months talking about, the name that friends embroidered on diaper bags, our first sons name, on a death certificate was chilling. In fact, it literally made me nauseous and made Brodie take his anger out on the hospital wall. It's interesting that seeing that our child is dead on paper seemed to make it so much more real, so much more final. The nurses brought Beau to us two or three times. By the third time his little features were starting to go soft, and I knew it was time to go.

Dr. Milligan had previously met with us to go over our options for the proceedings the next day. He asked us if we wanted an autopsy done on Beau. Brodie and I had no idea how to answer this question. I asked Dr. Milligan, what do people normally do under these circumstances. He assured me there is no normal here, but explained that if we wanted a better chance at getting answers an autopsy would be a good idea. Once you decide that you'd like to go ahead with an autopsy (a decision no parent should ever have to make regarding their child) you are then given a choice between two kinds, a full autopsy and a sort of minimal autopsy. Brodie and I put a lot of thought into this decision and decided on doing the full autopsy while telling ourselves we chose the latter.

The medical staff at our hospital really were incredible. One of the many kind things they did that day was take Beau's hand and footprints, and some clippings of his hair. We were given these keepsakes along with more hugs, and then, discharged.

CHAPTER 4
Guilt

 Leaving the hospital without our baby was one of the hardest parts of the whole process, and it was also a moment where I can pin point the wave of guilt that was about to crest. As we were walking out of the hospital, my husband gently asked nurse Alana if she was going to be there when Beau got picked up for transport. He asked if she could make sure someone was there with him and that they were gentle with our boy. As I placed one foot in front of the other it was as if I was walking into a new atmosphere where the oxygen was replaced with highly concentrated guilt…the kind of guilt that strangles you from the inside of your body. Why didn't I think to ask that? What kind of mother am I?

 The night to follow was the worst night. Brodie and I held each other while we cried and all I kept thinking was where is my baby? Should I have gone with him? Is he all-alone? I remember getting up in the middle of the night and walking into Beau's room, and collapsing on the spare bed in there. I also remember Brodie only a few steps behind me, picking me up, and bringing me back to our bed. I really can't describe to you how wonderful my husband is. Without him this journey would have been unbearable.

 Even though the people closest to me all told me this wasn't my fault the guilt took on a life of its own. I washed the floor one of the nights before I stopped feeling movement and as I would lay down some nights I would see newspaper headlines that said "MOM KILLS BABY BY WASHING FLOOR." I kid you not…they were in caps as they scrolled across my head. Even once the doctors told me there was no possible way cleaning the floor could have killed my baby I quickly jumped to a new scenario that was again my fault. Perhaps it was the few yoga classes I went to, or that one hot dog I ate. Maybe I didn't ask enough questions at my doctor's appointments. I was the only person in the world who could advocate for my baby and I let him down. How did I not know that he was in distress? How did I not know that he died? Of course, this wasn't my fault. As terrifying as it is to know, the truth is that sometimes babies die, and it's no one's fault, and it couldn't have been predicted, or prevented.

I never did feel like I wanted to blame anything or anyone other than myself in those early days, and I have come to truly believe I did not cause this, and I am not to blame. Brodie, my Mom, Gini, and my aunt Shelia are all owed a great deal of credit here, for helping me come to this life saving realization in the early days of my grief.

My mother in-law, Gini, lovingly stayed with Brodie and I in the days to come. Brodie's brother Clint, and his wife Jess, and Gini made it back to our house before us and they were quick to take down, or hide some of the baby things we had out and ready. For the next several days we did not leave our home. We cried, and we hurt, and we searched for answers.

After three days of not letting the sun touch our skin, Gini convinced Brodie and I to sit in the backyard with her and breathe in some fresh air. We live in a century home that we renovated this past year. It is right in the heart of our town and so the sidewalk in our front yard is very close to our home, and to our fenced in backyard. What this means is that people will often be walking by having a conversation or be talking on their phone and not realize we can hear every word they are saying. On this particular day, as Gini, Brodie, and I sat in silence, unsure if we would ever smile again a stranger was walking her dog along the sidewalk. She clearly did not know people were behind the nearby fence and was on the phone. She shouted "I am so DONE with your dog….she shit in the house and she's shitting again." "Angel you are disgusting! Stop peeing on everything!" Forget about smiling, we all belly laughed. We laughed and we kept laughing and it felt good. Thank you Gini, thank you stranger, and thank you Angel. Something that I learned a few years ago is that happiness and sadness are not on the same spectrum. That is, they move independently of each other. In that moment, I also learned that you can laugh, and be brave, and strong, and broken all at the same time.

I was still trying to decide when and how I would tell my parents. I did not want them to cut their trip short as I knew there was nothing they could do, and I figured they could join us in our grief when they got home. I talked to my brother Dylan a lot about when I should tell them and we decided it would be best to call them while they were at their hotel room in Athens the night before they were to fly back to Canada. So I did just that. I remember Brodie giving me a big hug before I made the call, and I remember knowing I would feel better once they knew…if I was able to get it out. I went into Beau's room and sat on the bed, and I dialled the number. My Dad answered the phone and sounded so happy. I just remember saying "Hi Dad" and he responded with "What's wrong?"

"Of course this wasn't my fault. As terrifying as it is to know, the truth is that sometimes babies die, and it's no ones fault, and it couldn't be predicted or prevented."

- Katy E. Martin

"You can laugh and be brave and broken and strong all at the same time."

- Katy E. Martin

I think the only words I could muster were "We lost our baby boy." I remember hearing my mom scream in the background. I reassured them that I was physically ok and that was pretty much the end of the phone call. We communicated via text in the hours that followed making a plan for them to fly straight to Manitoba once they landed in Toronto. I felt better after I had told my parents, but I also felt terrible knowing that I had just ruined their incredible trip. I also felt incredibly guilty that they didn't get to meet my son, or hold him, or talk to him. He is a part of them, and they never got those moments. *Lesson two that Beau taught me:* I do not have control over external forces. I only have control over how I respond to them. And so, I have to forgive myself, and accept that this didn't happen.

CHAPTER 5
The Ceremony

    In the days to come the cards began to fill up our mailbox, and the local flower shop began to quadruple their daily business. I think it was only the second day that we were home when the funeral company called us and set up a meeting to make arrangements for Beau. It all seemed to be moving so quickly. As hard as it was to do things, having small tasks gave us something to focus on. Brodie and I met with Nathan, the owner of the funeral home the next day. Nathan is the kind of person who was meant for his job. He is a taller, fair-haired, young man whose gentleness will never be forgotten. He explained that we should go and pick out a plot, and that the funeral home would absorb several costs as the death of a child is at the wrong end of life. This meant a lot to us at the time because let's face it, funerals and all that go with them can cost a lot of money, and in a time of such deep grief, and such guilt, what parent is able to make the decision of how much they can afford to do to honour their dead child. By the way the word 'dead' is hard for me to use. I feel like there is so much finality to it. Maybe it's because this is all so fresh still, or maybe I'm crazy, but I don't feel that Beau is entirely dead. His body is very much not living, this I understand. But his soul, well that is something altogether different isn't it. A quote I once read said,

> **"There is no death. Only a change of worlds"** - CHIEF SEATTLE

    I don't know where Beau is, but I know he is somewhere. He exists just like you, and me, and the trees, and ladybugs, and the birds, and fish, and stars.

"His body is very much not alive, this I understand. But his Soul, well that is something altogether different isn't it."

— Katy E. Martin

"THERE IS NO DEATH JUST A CHANGE OF WORLDS"

— Chief Seattle

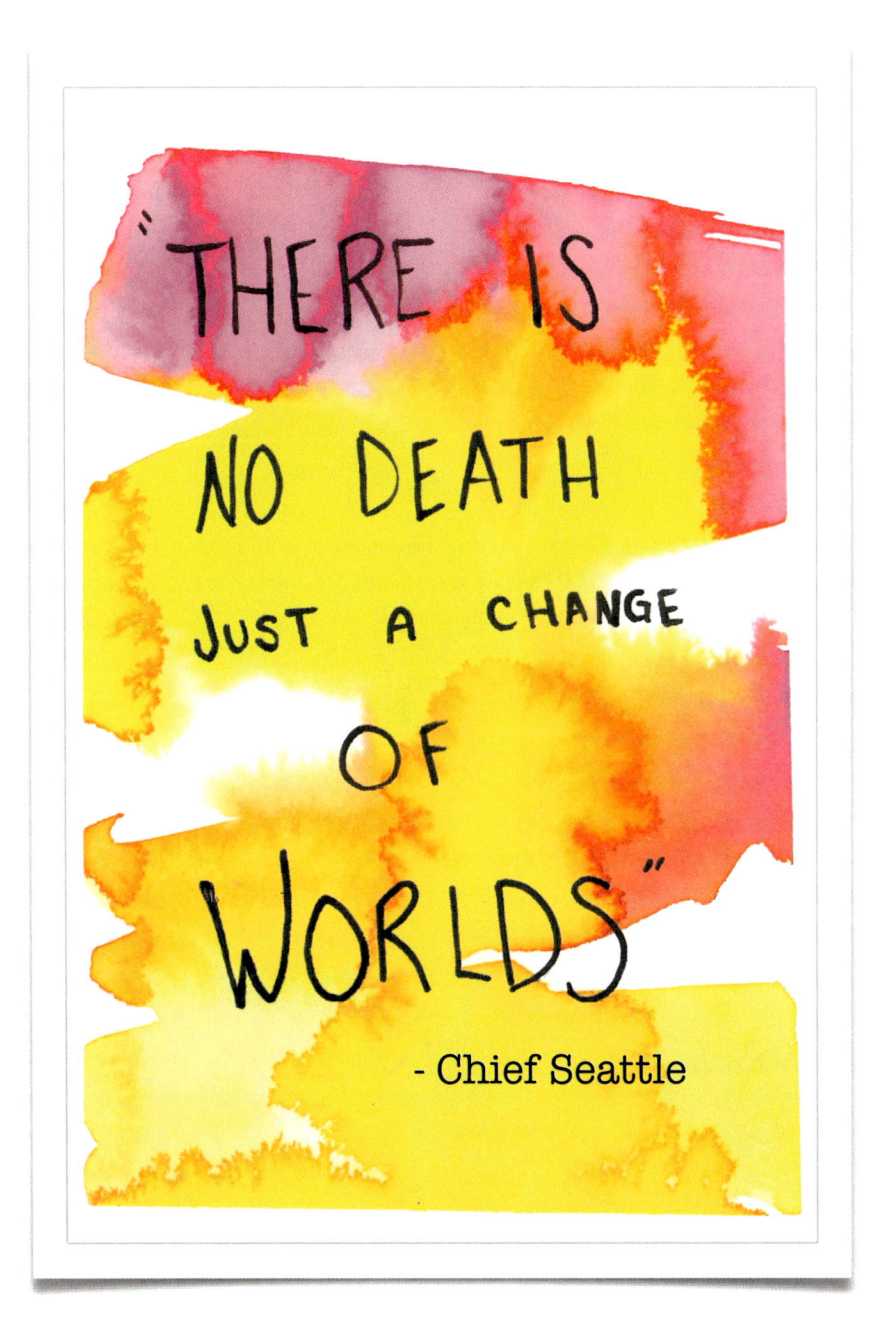

Seeing your child's name on a death certificate and having to sign it, choosing a burial plot for your brand new baby, picking out which baby urn to hold your infant's ashes, were all things that Brodie and I did not think we would be doing. Within a week I went from researching which stroller to buy to looking at headstones. Even as I am writing this it is an uncomfortable realization that the one constant in my behaviour before and after Beau was being a consumer. I realize that everything is a business but it was also shocking to hear things like, if you have your service on a weekend it will be $300.00, but if it is on a week day it will only cost $200.00. I hope one day we as humans will see the absurdity in all of this and some things will remain sacred instead of profitable.

Beau's day came and it went almost as quickly as he did. It was a beautiful day. I wrote some things down the day before that I wanted to say and so it went something like this:

I once read that grief never ends, but it changes. It's a passage, not a place to stay. Grief is not a sign of weakness, nor a lack of faith...it is the price of love and oh how you are loved our sweet baby Beau. I wish you could have seen the look on your Dad's face when he found out about you, or the pride in his eyes every time he felt you kick. I wish you knew how excited your grandparents were to meet you, and how much your Uncles and Aunts would have spoiled you. My Baby Beau, I carried you every second of your life and I will love you every second of mine. For all the things our hands ever held the best by far was you. You are not a 'lost pregnancy' or a 'stillborn.' You are not a sad thing that happened to us, or a tragic circumstance. You were our perfect baby boy and you still are; only while other babies learn to walk, our baby learns to fly. We will love you forever and look for you every night in the stars. XO Mom & Dad.

And ever so gently we lowered our perfect baby boy into the earth, and then we all went home.

Brodie started the day of Beau's funeral off by going to the Co-Op to buy lumber and built a butcher-block style counter for our laundry room. Brodie and I deal with our grief in different ways. It was apparent to me that he needed to keep physically busy. So I encouraged him to do so. The week after Beau died Brodie built a countertop, planted three medium sized trees in our yard, designed and constructed a deck, fixed the motor on our boat, and pushed gravel around half of our yard with a wheel barrel and shovel. I felt like I needed to get back to the earth so I joined Brodie in his busy grief.

"Grief never ends but it changes. It's a passage not a place to stay. Grief is not a sign of weakness nor a lack of faith It is the price of LOVE"

— Unknown

I spent one whole day after we lost Beau weeding the yard, brushing dirt off of the tree bark, watering the flowers, and raking leaves. It felt right to be touching the earth.

Another unfair reality of losing your baby on the last day of May was that Father's day seemed to approach with haste. Brodie and I both tried to pretend it didn't exist, that it wasn't a day to worry about, or put much thought into, but the truth is it stung, as did every upbeat Facebook post, every pregnant woman, every hospital room, every birth announcement, and baby stroller. This is a hard reality to swallow when only days before I was living in a world where I loved celebrating the success, milestones, and joys of others, and now I could barely let these events enter my consciousness. It's not that we weren't happy for other people, it's that seeing other people's happiness reminded us of how sad we were for us.

PART II
Summer

CHAPTER 6
Fight of Flight

  I consider myself to be a pretty analytical person. I am also a self-help junkie, and in true Katy style I turned to books and online articles for help in navigating this shattered heart that now lived inside of my somehow still breathing body. I read that during times of trauma our bodies typically respond with a fight or flight reaction. For me this was not a new concept and I was quite aware of my typical response. I had urges very early on for Brodie and I to pack our bags, and some food for our dog Piper, and for the three of us to hit the open road. One day while I was sitting by Beau's grave (even though I don't feel that he is there) I came to a realization. I felt that it was going to be profound for me and I needed to write it down. I'm not sure why it came out as a letter to my husband, but it did. And so I wrote....

  Brodie,

  You are my hero. I don't know how you do it, how you keep going, how you make me smile through the hardest days of our lives. Through all of this my most frequent thought is to run, for us to leave here, to leave our house, this town, the country...to disappear for a while. But for the first time today I had a different thought. What if we stay. What if we make our home a sanctuary. What if we go for a run to visit Beau every morning. What if we paddle the river every sunny day. What if we actually practice yoga, and meditation. What if we conquer our health through diet. What if we plan the best courses for the school year ahead. What if we learn to play the guitar and sit around the fire looking for him *in the stars. What if we create some incredible art together and put on a show that blows this town away. What if we stay, and Beau turns us into the people we always dreamed of being.*

And so we did just that. We stayed. We didn't conquer everything on our lists, but we did grow as people and the transformation that I feel I have participated in is mighty enlightening. In a yoga session that I attended at Landon's Legacy Retreat (a retreat for bereaved moms that I will talk about later) our instructor, and a person whose story, and efforts have been immeasurable in my own healing, and other bereaved mothers healing, Amelia Barnes said, "Maybe we should do less, and be more."

I feel as though that is what I did this summer. I became more. Beau has made me more. My heart was ripped into a million pieces over and over and over again. Every time I saw another baby, or pregnant woman, every hospital, every thought to the future, and all the recent memories of the past, broke it again, and again. Even the beautiful weather that we were having in Manitoba seemed to stab at the heart because I was supposed to be outside with my beautiful baby boy in those blissful summer days. But, what I have learned is that it made me feel sad, but it hasn't made me feel weak, or sorry for myself, or damaged. In fact, it has strengthened me, and awoken something deep inside that I did not know was there. I read this incredibly powerful poem by Julie Santiago and I felt myself relating to every single syllable.

"My heart was torn open into a hundred pieces two months ago, but not just because I was sad. It was torn open as I learned to feel even more. My heart held grief and love in a way that I never knew could co-exist. To witness the miracle of my body, the beauty of being a woman, and the strength and resilience of my spirit blew me away. I am different. Clear. Focused. Fierce. Tender. I am more me than I've ever been before. A new rite of passage. A new opportunity to deepen within myself. In many ways this little spirit baby birthed me. I am no longer the same."   - JULIE SANTIAGO

I recently stumbled upon a poet whose words also echoed a similar sentiment. Her name is Victoria Erickson and if I could buy everyone one of her books, or works of art rather, I would. She writes,

"I love people who have been through adversity and heartache and obstacles as impossible as the sun itself. They usually make it out with hearts as warm as gold. Cores made of fire. Lives soaked with intention. Hope like another morning. They know how to start again - how to walk through walls with palms wide open, and how to begin at the edge, and the end. Those to me are the best people." - VICTORIA ERICKSON

    I suppose for Brodie and I, the staying was us choosing to fight. Instead of boarding a plane to an unknown land and attempting to distract ourselves with travel, we stayed and we faced our greatest fear head on.

CHAPTER 7
Fear and the Ultimate Gift

It has been almost four months since Beau was born, and in the last few weeks I have been feeling brighter than I have ever felt. I started feeling like I was lighter, and stronger and like I am in the midst of true transformation. While this is going on for me, I am confusing the hell out of my colleagues as they witness me smiling and floating through the staff room at work. At the same time an insightful friend from my past sent me a message. She wrote,

"Hey Miss Katy; just wanted to let you know I'm thinking of you both. Something 'Awesomely Spectacular' is in the works." She also wrote, *"Katy, don't ever feel that you are in a 'fragile state' now…it's quite the opposite, actually…What you and Brodie have lived through (more-so YOU)…in some cultures, an experience like that is looked upon as an initiation of sorts. You've physically and spiritually lived through a horrific experience without dying. The woman who wakes up every morning now, Miss Katy – is a true warrior. With every day you will find yourself gaining more and more strength spiritually and physically. You have been given an even greater insight and awareness into people, their lives and their true intentions behind their words and actions. The experience of going through a loss like yours has honed your psyche like no other. You might still feel a bit squeaky, need some oiling, and some bolts are a bit loose…but as a whole, Katy there is a strength in you that is unmatched by any of your friends…You might even sketch or paint how you see yourself now…that would be pretty special!"*

This message began to validate some of the positive yet confusing feelings I was having. It also made me feel as though I was on the right path, as I had just a few days' prior, booked myself in for a private art show in Neepawa, even though I had no idea what the show would be about.

A lot of people are driven more by fear than anything else and before losing Beau I was no different. I don't think you can even contemplate how many of your daily decisions are made out of fear until life places your biggest fears directly in front of you. Yet, the incredible thing about walking through your biggest fears is the gift of freedom on the other side. After Beau left us, I had a hard time explaining to people this exact phenomenon. The feelings I was having didn't add up to what I thought I should be feeling. I felt fearless, I felt lighter, I felt at peace, yet I also felt shame and guilt for feeling these things, for gaining anything positive from my son's death. Even though my insightful friend had begun to validate my positive feelings, I still felt uneasy about them and ultimately confused. And then, I found a very special book.

Mo Gawdat is the Chief Business Officer at Google's [X]. Despite his incredible success, he was deeply unhappy, and so he applied his engineering analysis to every component of happiness. In doing so he came up with a kind of equation for happiness in a book he wrote called *Solve for Happy*. What I didn't know when I picked this book up was that Mo too had lost his son, and thus many of his feelings were directly in line with mine. Mo's son's name was Ali, and he died due to a medical mistake during a fairly routine procedure at the age of 21. Mo writes in-depth about his experience of losing his son and his words not only helped to validate the space that I was in, but helped bring clarity to my confusion. Mo states,

"When Ali left, I died, and I say that in the most positive sense. Life finally fit into perspective. I have an overwhelming feeling of peace. There is nothing more to lose; there is nothing more to fear. Eckhart Tolle says this is "to die before you die," to live life knowing that because one day it'll all be gone, there's really nothing that you have and so nothing you have to lose. I cry every time I remember that the price for my freedom was his life. But Ali too has found his path. He too is at peace…There isn't a single day in life worth living in fear." - MO GAWDAT

Ah ha! This is precisely what I was feeling, yet couldn't accurately describe. My body seemed to absorb this understanding so naturally that in the depths of my grief when I would lay beside my husband in bed I remember thinking, right now you are warm, and safe, and in a comfortable bed, in a beautiful home, laying beside the man you love the most, and to breathe all of this in, because all of this, will one day, be gone too. I suppose to some people that could seem depressing but really it isn't. To know that nothing lasts forever, that all you have is this moment and even this moment is unpredictable. It frees you. It makes you soak up every idle hour. It reminds you to cherish the things in front of you that you love. It allows you to let things go, and to set others free. And, for those who feel they have even less because perhaps they are going through something like this alone please remember,

"Tonight, you may be sorrowful or silent, empty or alone, but you have the moon, and you have your breath, and in inhaling the wonder of these alone, you might find yourself wrapped in the shawl of gentle relief that this very moment is beautiful, and more than worthy of perfect love." - VICTORIA ERICKSON

I don't know if it is possible for one to come to this kind of peace without being brought to your knees from a loss of this magnitude. I hope that some people can come to this profound understanding through their own self work and through stories of others. But I also hope that for those who do find themselves face to face with a fear like this, that they know, there is a gift waiting for them. A gift that may have taken them a lifetime to learn otherwise. A gift that will enrich the rest of their life. A gift that will answer the big questions, that will put their life into perspective, that will increase their frequency on this planet. The ultimate gift of inner peace.

CHAPTER 8
Suffering

 This week my close friend Alexa purchased the book, *Landon's Legacy* for me, written by Amelia Kathryn Barnes (the yoga instructor and retreat facilitator I mentioned earlier). So much of what Amelia wrote resonated with me. As I continued reading I discovered Amelia was not only Canadian, but lived in Manitoba just two hours away. I also discovered she facilitates a retreat for Mom's like me called Landon's Legacy Retreat.

 It seems the stars aligned, as they say, and everything fell into place for me to go to this retreat. I told Brodie that day in the car, as I was reading Landon's Legacy, that I knew I was supposed to go to this, that I was supposed to go this year. I checked it out online, and the retreat was only a week away. I tried to register and realized it was also already full. Brodie tried to comfort me suggesting it would be great for me to go next year, but I told him I needed to go now. In my determination I found Amelia on Facebook that evening and reached out to her, sharing my story and expressing my desire to attend. The next day Amelia responded saying,

 "Hi Katy…I'm getting total goose bumps reading this. Thank you, thank you for writing. I would love to meet you and hear all about your precious Beau. Crazy things-I rarely check my other FB inbox but I did today. AND one of the moms attending this year's retreat just cancelled because of a complicated pregnancy, would you like to come?"

 I emailed my Superintendent at 10pm that evening explaining the retreat and my strong feelings about being at it. He responded at 10:03pm with approval. Interestingly enough his son is also named Landon. 'Crazy things' is right.

 I work for, in my opinion, one of the best school divisions in Canada, and my Principal met with my Superintendent the following morning sorting out my leave. I packed my bag that weekend and got a ride from a new friend Erin who lives in Brandon and who like all of us Mama's, tragically lost her son, Arlo, late in pregnancy. Some amazing things happened at this retreat. I met my tribe. A group of women so strong, that being in their presence brings you to tears. I looked within, I wrote, I cried, I breathed deep, and for the first time I really reflected on all that had happened. I think this is a very important part of grieving. The leaning in. The feeling every single crumb.

"When there's a fresh wound in your heart, keep it open until it heals. Air it out. Understand it. Dive into it. Be fierce enough to become it. If you ignore it, it won't be able to breathe. If you ignore it it will merely deepen, spread and resurface later wanting to release. And when later happens, it will hurt even more, because when later happens, you won't know what you're bleeding for. Remain with it until it clears, and watch the beauty pour into your openness. Remain open to feel lightness. Remain open to feel free."
- VICTORIA ERICKSON

Lesson three that Beau taught me: The valleys of my emotions are deep, and I will not fear them.

Years ago I watched a documentary on a teenage boy who was diagnosed with cancer. His Mom said in part of her interview that the gift of cancer was that life is richer, colours are brighter. Even then it resonated with me, but I now have lived what she meant. I think that some people can go through their entire lives not knowing what it means to cherish every single moment. Not knowing what it's like rushing home on a week night to watch the sunset from your roof or to listen to good music really loudly and let it fill every corner of your body or to feel true gratitude every single night that they lay in their warm comfortable bed beside their loving partner, or when they surrender and are sobbing from deep heartache that they realize how lucky they are to have strong lungs and clean air to fill them with. *Lesson four that Beau taught me:* the gift of tragedy is that life is richer. I am so grateful for this lesson, and every day I thank Beau.

Today in a mindfulness class at the retreat, we were asked to answer a question. *If I were to give up wanting this to be different, what would I lose, what would I gain, and what would I learn.*

"The valleys of my emotions are deep... and I will not fear them"

— Katy E. Martin

"The gift of tragedy is that Life is richer"

— Katy E. Martin

"IF I WERE TO GIVE UP WANTING THIS TO BE DIFFERENT, WHAT WOULD I LOSE, WHAT WOULD I GAIN, AND WHAT WOULD I LEARN."

- Unknown

While I was doing some researching on suffering I read that in Buddhist culture they understand that your suffering is not holding you, you are holding your suffering. I recognize this and I believe this. Yet, I came to the theory that suffering was all that I had of Beau. I do not have him here with me so what would happen if I let go of that suffering. I wrote that maybe I would lose some closeness to him. Maybe I would gain some peace. Maybe I would learn that suffering does not bring closeness and is not a measure of how much we love.

Before I came to this realization, suffer I did. I wanted to suffer, and I wanted the whole world, and everyone in it to suffer with me. I wanted to look out the window and see storm clouds. I wanted the thunder to crack down and the sky to pour rain. I wanted it to be dark outside, and I wanted to cry, and cry, and drink water so that I could cry even more. I remember waking up in the middle of the night and realizing that I had bled through my pyjamas. It gave me another thing to be upset about, and so I changed my clothes and decided to sleep, for the rest of the night, on our couch in the living room. I needed to steady my mind so I turned on the TV, and fell asleep to its hum. I woke up to the sound of bagpipes, and candy being thrown at my window. At first, I thought the noise was coming from the TV but I quickly realized it had shut off. I scratched my head, and stood up from the couch in nothing but my t-shirt, and underwear. I heard bagpipes because there were men playing bagpipes marching down the street, along with floats, and balloons, and fire trucks, and children cheering, and sirens, and literally happiness, and celebration whisking by in the perfectly formed clouds in the very sunny sky. Not only did I wake up to people sitting on my lawn watching the parade I quickly realized our corner lot home was the marker for where the parade turned so we got to see it literally wrap around our house. I'm sure the irony here is pretty apparent. For Brodie and I time had stopped. Our whole world had changed, and we were deep in our grief, yet the rest of the world not only carried on with daily life but, celebrated. To make things even more ironic the very next day I woke up, again on the couch, and again to an even bigger parade. Apparently we had moved to the town that's known for its parades.

"The worst possible thing in the world can happen and the morning will come. The sun will rise same as it ever has. You'll gaze out the window. You'll stir your tea. All is well. And will be." -VICTORIA ERICKSON

Mo Gawdat also talks a lot about suffering in his book, *Solve for Happy* that I referenced earlier. Just like the Buddhists he proclaims that,

"It's the thought, not the actual event, that's making you unhappy." - MO GAWDAT

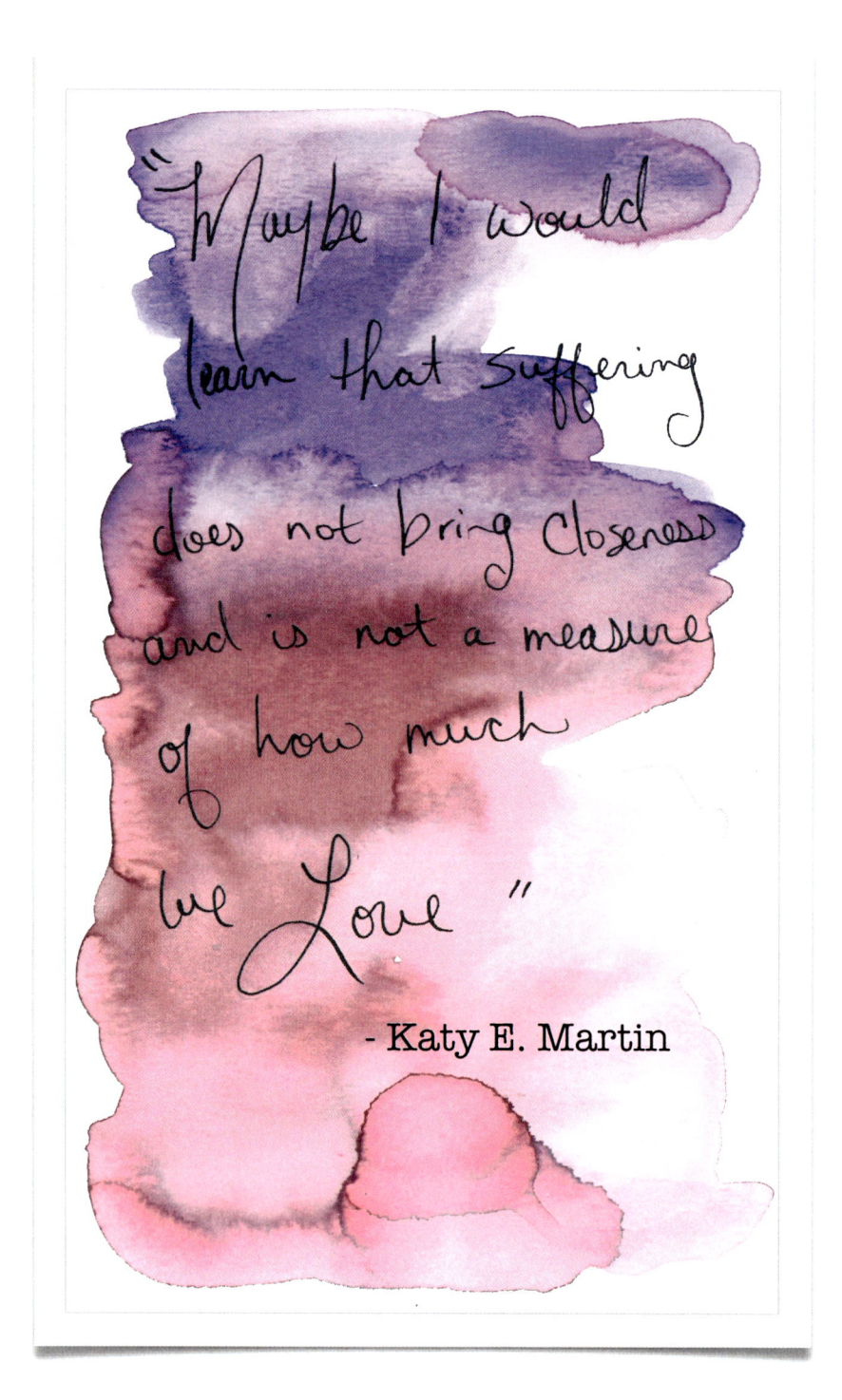

"Maybe I would learn that suffering does not bring closeness and is not a measure of how much we Love."

- Katy E. Martin

And that,

"Suffering offers no benefit whatsoever. None!" - MO GAWDAT

But the analogy he gives regarding this is what I liked best. Mo states that,

"The interesting thing is, just as we have the ability to engage in our suffering at will, we also have the ability to debug our pain systems if we put our minds to it. But we don't always make that choice. Imagine that you need a root canal and the dentist offers you either (a) the standard procedure with a few days of recovery or (b) a root canal with additional bonus days of extensive excruciating pain. Why on earth would you ever go with (b)?" - MO GAWDAT

Yet people choose this every day. They choose to prolong their pain, to punish themselves with longer, deeper suffering. Mo continues to write,

"The day my wonderful son left, everything went dark. I felt I had earned the right to suffer for the rest of my life, that I was given no choice but to close my door and decay. I was, in reality, given two choices: (a) I could choose to suffer for the rest of my life and it would not bring Ali back, or (b) I could choose to feel the pain but stop the miserable thoughts, do all that I could to honour his memory, and it would still not bring Ali back—though it would make the world just a little bit easier to endure." - MO GAWDAT

After losing our son Beau, I instinctively chose (b). I don't know why that was my choice from so early on, or why some people have a much more difficult time seeing the choices in front of them. I do know that reading about others making a conscious effort to choose not to suffer gave me the boost I needed to continue on my path of making my loss beautiful, of making it meaningful and of choosing inner peace. I came across some folks who would tell me that I wasn't crying enough, or that this wasn't a time for me to be strong. I am grateful for Mo Gawdat's insight, and wisdom, and for stumbling upon his golden nugget of a book, *Solve for Happy*, just when I did.

PART III
Fall

CHAPTER 9
A Parking Spot on Pegasus

So it's mid-October now, and the last few weeks have been particularly sharp. I'm not sure why but what I've learned about grief is that it is certainly not linear. I think that in the beginning of losing Beau, there was so much to experience. This was my first real tragedy, the first time I'd gone through labor, the first time I'd seen a dead body, the first time I'd seen a dead baby, the first time I'd held a dead baby. Then there was the logistics of planning a funeral, choosing a plot, and picking the font for a head stone.

After that I was dealing with the healing of my body, and the true loss of identity I felt. I read in one of the grief pamphlets that was given to me, that when you are pregnant there is a trauma to your body, and when you lose a baby you move directly from that trauma to the trauma of the loss of your child, and then directly to the trauma of the loss of self. It has taken time to work through all of the experiences, the tasks, and then the feelings, and it feels like I am just now realizing that I have lost my son. That I will never get to fill his stocking that I bought him last December. I am realizing I will never get to choose a Halloween costume for Beau, or give him a bath, or buy him a toy. I will never get to mother this baby in any of the ways that I thought I was supposed to. I'm not sure how I will be able to mother him now, but I hope to find ways on special days and in simple moments.

I'm still not exactly sure what my beliefs are regarding the afterlife, but I do know and have known for some time now, that my sweet baby is somewhere safe, and warm, and happy. I also think that wherever he is he is busy. I'm not sure what he is doing but he is the furthest thing from static, or still, or lifeless, or stuck in the ground. I know this with such certainty that my own death is much less fearful. And since I see our Beau somewhere in the sky, and in the spaces in between, I had a moment where I did in fact feel motherly. It was the first thing that felt meaningful enough to do in Beau's memory, and that was to buy him, a star. I always loved the quote;

"We have calcium in our bones, iron in our veins, carbon in our souls, and nitrogen in our brains. We are 93 percent stardust, with souls made of flames, we are all just stars that have people names." – NIKITA GRILL

Every time I read it I feel closer to Beau. As soon as our star arrived I searched for meaning in its placement and to my surprise found our Beau star among the Pegasus constellation in the Northern Hemisphere. Yes! We bought our boy a parking spot on Pegasus. For those of you that haven't brushed up on your Greek mythology,

"Pegasus...was involved in some of the most intriguing tales of the times. From his birth to his death, Pegasus remained a mysterious creature capable of everything, symbolizing the divine inspiration or the journey to heaven, since riding him was synonymous to "flying" to the heavens. Pegasus was represented as a goodhearted, gentle creature, somewhat naive but always eager to help. For his service and loyalty, Zeus honoured him with a special immortality turning Pegasus into a constellation on the last day of his life." - Greekmyths-greekmythology.com

I don't suppose any constellation would be as meaningful as this one, and I love looking for it in the sky and thinking about Beau flying to the heavens and shining above us forever.

Speaking of a special day…it was Brodie's birthday this weekend, and I decided with the dark days we had just wandered through, that maybe some time recharging amongst the trees would be a good retreat for us both. So, we packed up our car, and my Mom graciously cooked us an entire turkey dinner for the road. We drove to Riding Mountain National Park, and decided to set up our tent beside Whirlpool Lake. It was Thanksgiving weekend, minus three degrees outside, and a pretty secluded little campsite. As you can imagine we did not expect to see anyone else at the site and were looking forward to the quiet of nature. We ate our dinner, watched the sunset and tucked ourselves into bed under three sleeping bags and a comforter.

"We have calcium in our bones, iron in our veins, carbon in our souls and nitrogen in our brains. We are 93% STAR DUST with souls made of flames, we are all just STARS with people names."

— Nikita Gill

We fell asleep to the sound of the fire crackling, and the wind blowing. It was very peaceful, and quite romantic, until around 4am when a flock of over one hundred Canadian geese landed beside our tent, and honked for what felt like hundreds of years. Again, thank you sweet baby Beau for teaching me that life is unpredictable, and that control is an illusion.

CHAPTER 10
The Fragility of Life

    People talk a lot about anxiety and wonder how I would go through another pregnancy without being driven crazy with worry. The truth is if we are lucky enough to conceive again, I don't know what I will be like. I know that in the early days after losing Beau my anxiety was high. I worried as I lay in bed beside Brodie that I would not be able to go back to work in two months because I would be apart from him, a thought I couldn't bare at the time. I spent an afternoon on our friends, Kathy and Graham's, boat and their youngest daughter Sadie crawled on my lap, and fell asleep. She was probably asleep for almost an hour, and I put my hand under her life jacket close to twenty times checking to see if she was breathing. I felt that just being near me could somehow cause her to stop breathing. The anxiety was real, and it was strong. That's kind of what happens when you witness first -hand the fragility of life, when you understand that babies can die, children can die, the person you love the very most in this world can, and will die. *Lesson five that Beau has taught me:* all relationships have a time limit. Once you truly come to understanding this you will realize that we do not get to choose how long our children will live, we only get to love them. This notion is both freeing, and utterly terrifying.

    On the downswings of my grief I felt like I was truly broken, empty, less desirable. On the upswings I felt brighter, and stronger, and that maybe broken pieces weren't the worst thing to have. Maybe broken pieces were the beginning of a whole new work of art.

"All relationships have a time limit."

— Katy E. Martin

"Maybe broken pieces were the begining of a whole new Work of ART."

— Katy E. Martin

CHAPTER 11
Beau Bears

  Not long after losing Beau we had to travel back to Ontario for some doctor's visits. We had the immense pleasure of going to dinner with my cousin Ryan and his lovely wife Jaclyn. Over roasted cauliflower appetizers we listened to their story as they too tragically lost their baby girl this past summer not long after delivery. Jaclyn and Ryan were given a stuffed bear to leave with, donated by parents who had also lost a child. Brodie and I decided we loved this idea and we wanted to purchase some bears with a little note on them, to be dropped off at local hospitals, for parents like us. Also how cute does *Beau Bear* sound, right!? So we did just that. I signed into my Vista Print account, wrote an extreme Coles Notes version of our story, and on a special day we dropped the bears off at the hospital where we delivered Beau. I wrote a letter to Beau, and posted it with our Beau Bear photos on Facebook to not only remember our son on the day he would have been six months old, but to also spread awareness.

  Beau,

  Today you would have been a whopping six months old. I wonder what you would be like if you were here. I wonder how hard your nephews would have had you giggling this Christmas. I miss your ten long fingers and your ten little toes. I miss those perfect lips and that button nose. I miss the weight of you in my arms and your blonde surfer curls. Each day that passes I miss you even more. I need you to know that it's ok that you aren't here. I will never understand it, but I accept that you had other places to be, and other jobs to do. I know now that some lives aren't meant to be long but they are meant to be BIG. Your life has touched so many others, and your memory will live on through us, that I can promise you. By the way your Dad is still jealous of your hair! Ohh and Piper still sleeps in your room every chance she gets. Today we dropped off the first Beau Bears at the hospital! These bears are to be given to parents like us, to comfort them and to tell them all about you! Even in your short life you have made your parents so proud, in all of the lessons you've given to so many different lives. You've taught me more in a single moment than I maybe would have learned in a lifetime. Shine bright over this magical season Baby. I will love you forever, and ever, and ever, and ever, and after that too. XO Mom"

"Some lives aren't meant to be long, but they are meant to be BIG"

— Amelia Kathryn Barnes

PART IV
Winter

CHAPTER 12
The Christmas Stocking

It's now the last day of January. My son would have been a very exciting eight months old today had he stayed instead of heading back to the stars. A few months have passed since I last wrote, and really a lot has happened. The dreaded first Christmas without him, came and went, quite quickly, thank goodness. I kept telling myself it's just another day and it wouldn't be that hard. I was wrong. It was hard. It felt empty, it felt pointless, it felt cold. Last December when I was pregnant, and my naive heart was full of love, I was shopping and I wanted to buy our new little family some beautiful stockings. Stockings have always been my favourite part of Christmas. I found beautiful soft faux fur stockings. Mine was all white, Brodie's was mostly brown, and Beau's was a mixture of white and brown which seemed more than fitting. This year I didn't know what to do with his stocking. I hung it up beside mine and Brodie's, (the only décor I begrudgingly installed) but every time I looked at it I would start to cry. I didn't want his stocking to make us cry. I had to flip this onto its head in some way. So I thought about it for a long time and I came up with an idea. I decided that on Christmas Eve, whoever was with us, or whoever wanted to, could write down their happiest or funniest memories of the year in a short note to Beau. Of course it didn't need to be a feather-quilled letter, but just some genuinely funny or lovely moments. I asked my family to participate, and of course they did. Everyone took a moment to write something. We put all of the notes into an envelope and dated it 2017. We sealed it up without reading anyone's writings. Now, next year on Christmas Eve, we will be excited to see his stocking and to read aloud the funny moments from the Christmas before. My hope is that as our families grow, Beau's stocking will be a fuzzy vault, a type of treasure trove, of our best and happiest family memories. All in all, I can't say we enjoyed the season, but we did survive it, and I am proud of the beauty we were able to bring to a once somber stocking.

CHAPTER 13
The Medium

One of the moms I met at the retreat told me about a medium session she had that blew her away, and helped to give her some closure about the loss of her son. I had never had a medium session before, but I was always intrigued by the idea of going. So I asked my friend Sunshine, a veteran medium goer, to suggest one. She did, and Brodie and I made our way there. Our reading was very accurate, and quite frankly broke my husband's mind wide open on the topic. She explained to us that souls are created perfect, and that it is our human bodies that are often quite flawed. She told us that Beau's body wasn't ready yet, even though his soul was, and that he would be back. She told us that we would have a beautiful daughter, and a son in the future, that we would be busy with real estate, but live in our home for a long time. She said over, and over that I was meant to be a teacher, and that Brodie would do well with land. I did take some comfort in her words, and I do think about them often. She also told us that astrologically speaking, last year was all about endings, and that ultimately it was bad timing, but that 2018 was all about new beginnings.

CHAPTER 14
Courage

It was a full moon, and the very first day of the New Year, and I was late. I have a very regular cycle, and so I knew what this meant. Of course, I didn't have any pregnancy tests in our house, and because of the holiday everything in our small town was closed. So, first thing the next morning, Brodie and I drove to Brandon, we stopped at a pharmacy, picked up a test, and pulled into the first café we saw. I went into the public washroom, and even though I had maybe three drops of pee to push out, that stick turned into a plus sign almost instantly. I guess the medium was right about 2018 being about new beginnings. I came out smiling and Brodie knew.

So I've been pregnant now for two months. My mind has run away with my thoughts, and I often feel like I'm just a vessel for them to run amuck in. We still have no answers about what happened to Beau, and by now we know we probably never will. I tell myself that it must have been a cord accident, and surely we won't be struck by lightning twice. I repeat to myself that so many women have had a loss, and then gone on to have healthy strong babies. I remind myself that this is a different pregnancy, a different baby, and a different story with a different ending. But I also know that I have met some incredible women that have gone through this more than once, and who also have no answers. I know that I have a chance of being both the former and the latter. More than anything, I know that I have to make my baby and I one. I must choose to create peace within me, and around me. With statistics, and unanswered questions, our history has set the stage for possible negative outcomes in our future. It is because I may only get twelve weeks, or eight months with this baby that I feel a duty to show him/her the beauty of life. I will laugh every single hour; I will flood their cells with evergreen scented oxygen. I will eat every single colour of the rainbow in its most raw form.

"This is a different pregnancy, a different baby a different story with a different ending."

- Unknown

This baby will never know fear or guilt or shame. This baby will read only the best literature, listen to only the greats, and be spoken to about only the best ideas. I don't have control over everything, this I am now very aware of. But, what I can control, you better believe I will. The truth is I might not get to bring this baby home either. This baby might be buried beside their brother Beau at our town's cemetery, on the top of the valley, overlooking the lake. This is not planning to fail. This is the painful wisdom that comes with trauma and loss. This is planning to be successful here and now, in this very moment, in the only moment we have. Because right now, as I write this, I am pregnant, and my baby is alive, and strong. And so, it is up to me to decide if my strong, and very much living baby will feel fear or joy, will hear their mom cry or laugh, will feel stress or sense the forest.

So I lived large in happiness, and large in love. I spent eleven weeks laughing, eating incredibly well, and walking in the crisp winter air. But this time I didn't get eight months, or even twelve weeks. I got to celebrate being pregnant for eleven weeks, and then our pregnancy came to an end. Our baby vanished as quickly as they came. And this time we didn't get to know them, or feel their hiccups, or even choose their name. Quickly my mind was brought to the quote,

"Courage doesn't always roar. Sometimes courage is the quiet voice at the end of the day saying I will try again tomorrow." - MARY ANNE RADMACHER

And so, we will try again tomorrow.

"Courage doesn't always roar. Sometimes courage is the quiet voice at the end of the day saying "I will try again tomorrow."

- Mary Anne Radmacher

CHAPTER 15
Attitude & Perspective

This morning while I was sipping a giant cup of perfectly steeped tea, I read another quote, one that I feel is so simple yet so true. The quote read,

"The most important decision you will ever make is to be in a good mood." - VOLTAIRE

Gretchen Rubin is a self-help book rock star, and her book *The Happiness Project* was my bible for a year or so. Keep in mind this was before I had ever experienced any kind of true loss. In fact, Brodie purchased the book for me when we had first started dating, while we were at an airport, because I was feeling blue, and was struggling with getting over a pretty straight forward break up. Gretchen dedicated a year of her life to researching happiness, and her findings are incredibly helpful. To help people improve their lives she has come up with commandments, one being **"Act the way I want to feel."** She explains **"This commandment sums up one of the most helpful insights that I'd learned in my happiness research: although we presume that we act because of the way we feel, in fact we often feel because of the way we act. For example, studies show that even an artificially induced smile brings about happier emotions."** In the book Gretchen talks about this technique more to help people boost their energy. She talks about acting energetic to feel like you have more energy, and gives good evidence of how this really works.

I use this strategy regularly, and I found it especially helpful getting through the first year after losing Beau. I knew that I didn't want Beau's life to be a dark cloud that brought tears, and heaviness.

"The most important decision you will ever make is to be in a good mood."

— Voltaire

So on days when I felt heavy I would think of a way to celebrate Beau, or an activity that would alter my mindset. I would let myself feel the emotion, and I'd usually have an intense but fairly quick cry, leaning into the emotion, but then I'd go for a walk, or bake some bread, or go get a tea, or call a friend, or find a comedian on TV. Really, this seems quite simple. We all know how to cheer a downtrodden kid up, but I think as adults sometimes we forget to cheer ourselves up. Sometimes we decide we should stew in our sadness, or act sad because we feel sad. We forget to act happy perhaps not knowing that it can actually make us feel happy. I also made sure to dress up for work. The old, look good, feel good trick, and you know what, it helped too. If you read a little further in her book she quotes G.K. Chesterton, **"It is easy to be heavy: hard to be light."** This quote has always resonated deeply with me, and I try to remember it when I notice myself spinning downward. I think Victoria Erickson speaks of this also when she writes,

"Dwelling on the negative merely lowers your vibration and creates sickness in the mind and body. Use your internal strength and willpower to rise above the thoughts pulling you down and watch your world rise alongside you, continuing to meet you exactly where you are." -VICTORIA ERICKSON

Everyone is very sad for us, and I'm sure they want to wrap us up in their arms, and take away our pain. The truth is, I am of course disappointed. But really I'm feeling ok. I've bought into the idea of this being my road, and of choosing to be happy, and for me, it's really working. It has changed my attitude, and my perspective, and I feel positive a lot more than I feel negative. When I think about it logically, I think that we have ten good years of trying ahead of us, and I already know we can conceive, and that I can carry a baby to term. So I am confident that it will work out, and that whatever baby is on their way, they are preparing us to be incredibly strong people whose optimism cannot be shaken, and whose love is beyond fierce.

My mom was reading a book that has been around for quite some time called *Man's Search for Meaning* by Viktor E. Frankl. She just so happened to leave it on my coffee table and said I'd probably enjoy it. I started reading

it before I got the news that we were going to miscarry, and somehow it was the PERFECT piece of literature to be reading during that time. Viktor was an Austrian neurologist and psychiatrist who survived several concentration camps during the Holocaust. In the first half of the book he describes his time in the camps, and the second half he delves into his theories on how humans find meaning. He dedicated the latter years of his life to helping people see the meaning behind their suffering, and changing people's attitudes about their circumstances. He explains that once a person can see a reason for their suffering they no longer suffer, their situation becomes endurable. A quote from his book that tugged at my heart was that, "...**love is as strong as death.**" Prior to this sentence, Viktor spoke of the unbearable conditions that he and the other men were living in. Yet, his reason for describing how bad the conditions were, was not to evoke sympathy from his readers, but to illuminate a truth that he discovered. In the depths of their despair, their minds would wander to their wives and they would be elated living in that thought if only for a moment. He writes,

"For the first time in my life I saw the truth...that love is the ultimate and highest goal to which man can aspire." He continues, **"I understood how a man who has nothing left in this world still may know bliss, be it only for a brief moment, in the contemplation of his beloved."** - VIKTOR E. FRANKL

While Viktor was in the trenches, freezing from frostbite, his mind numb from horror, malnourishment, and extreme abuse, still, he writes,

"My mind still clung to the image of my wife. A thought crossed my mind: I didn't even know if she were still alive. I knew only one thing-which I have learned well by now: Love goes very far beyond the physical person of the beloved. It finds its deepest meaning in his spiritual being, his inner self. Whether or not he is actually present, whether or not he is still alive at all, ceases somehow to be of importance." - VIKTOR E. FRANKL

CHAPTER 16
Your Road

I know that our stories are all so different. I know that there will be people reading this who cannot conceive, or who cannot carry a baby to term, or people that have experienced a neonatal loss, or the loss of an older child, or some that may have had to terminate a pregnancy for the sake of the baby's quality of life. What I want you to know is that none of us can predict the future, and really who would want to anyways. I have to say, these certainly aren't the blissful family building years I had anticipated either. They aren't filled with relaxing pregnancies, cute baby bumps and even cuter maternity outfits. It isn't me and my friends sipping our decaffeinated teas and talking about the ease of our symptoms. It's a terrifying road with bends and bumps, with upsetting symptoms, and unimaginably difficult outcomes. It is grief filled, anxiety ridden, and belief changing. It isn't easy, and many days it doesn't seem fair. But it is OUR road. And so we shall continue down it, bumps, bends, morning sickness, somber ultrasounds, positive pee tests, and all. We will make our road a work of art. We will make our road beautiful.

In his book *Solve for Happy* Mo also talks more about this idealized thought of being positive, yet he describes it as looking down. He talks a lot about our success, and progress driven culture. He explains that if we are always looking up at what we don't have we will never be happy and that we need to start looking down. He writes,

"There's nothing wrong with wanting to advance in life, but looking up, to compare, will end in vain. There will always be a reason to feel that what you may have achieved is not good enough. Employees look up to managers, and managers look up to chief executives. Models look up to thinner supermodels, and millionaires look up to billionaires. Here's a challenge: Try reframing ambition so the focus is on the goal of becoming a better person regardless of how you compare to others. Even better, look down. Work hard, grow, and make a difference in the world, but please feel good about yourself. Please stop looking at what you don't have. What you don't have is infinite. Making that your reference point is a sure recipe for disappointment—and a sure way to fail the Happiness Equation. Instead of looking at the few who may appear to have more than you, look instead at the billions who have less. Yes—billions!" - MO GAWDAT

I think this lesson is important for all of us no matter where you're at in your life, and especially in today's constant comparing, selfie climate. I think this lesson is also very important for women who are trying to start their own families. Recently, I have had several friends reach out asking for advice or sometimes just needing someone to talk to about this heavy weight that they are carrying. This fear of not being able to conceive, of running into complications, and of having a loss. So this is what I've told them. This is my note on the family building years:

What I have learned is that even though it isn't the road you thought it would be, it is YOUR road, and there is no turning back or changing that. I have learned so much more from the tough stuff than I ever did the easy. We live in a time where there are so many ways that we can become parents. The options are plentiful, and even though it doesn't always feel fair, or like it should be THIS hard, all of the setbacks, challenges, and heartaches are molding you into an incredible parent, one who doesn't take the little moments for granted. One who doesn't argue with their husband about who stays in, and who goes out, or whose turn it is to change a diaper. Being pregnant is a beautiful thing, but we cannot deny there are sacrifices you make while pregnant, and your body really isn't your own. So I tell my friends every month that your heart sinks when you see that crimson red in the toilet...like Mo says, "**look down**" and use that moment as a time to celebrate the fact that you are menstruating, which is a sign of health not afforded to all women. Thank your body for all of the things that it is doing right. Change your attitude, and enjoy the rest of the month with your body being your own. Go and buy an expensive coffee, your favourite wine and chocolate, and enjoy them guilt free. Go and get a massage, or sit in someone's hot tub, or go to a spa. These are things you may not get to do when you do conceive, which in all likelihood, you will. And even if you hit road block after road block trying to build your family the old fashion way, I think there is something positively magical about a child growing in your heart instead of your body and adopting. Start making love to your partner for no other reason than pleasure. Remember that once you do have a small child, or baby in your house you and your partner won't have the time you have together now, so instead of being upset, enjoy those precious years. You will look back, and wish you wouldn't have fought your way through them. Being positive, and relaxed, and enjoying everything that you DO have won't (necessarily) make you conceive, but neither will being hard on yourself, or being stressed, or mad at your body. Life is hard either way, but you get to decide what this path of yours will look like...it's your road, make it beautiful. Mo made his path beautiful, and he explains,

"If I want to look up at how much longer we could have lived together, I would suffer because the fact is he left and there's nothing I can do about that. Instead, I choose to look down and feel grateful for the twenty-one wonderful years during which he blessed us with his presence. Instead of feeling resentful that he died, I feel grateful that he lived."
- MO GAWDAT

I feel this way about Beau, and about every future lively babe growing in my belly. No matter what happens, I feel grateful that I got to feel life inside of me, and that I got to hold my son. I'm not saying our roads will be easy. In fact, if you're reading this book I can almost guarantee your road hasn't been. But I have stood on some sacred ground with a group of incredible bereaved mothers, and I have felt their strength radiate the floorboards. It won't be easy but the inner strength that will penetrate your being, the perspectives you will gain, the tribe you will find, the peace you will feel, and the brightness of the colours that you will see, will make carrying on, oh so worth it.

PART V
Spring

CHAPTER 17
The Art Show

  Spring is in the air! I took Piper for a walk today and hearing the birds chirp, and seeing the sun melt some of our winter away brought a smile to my face. Since I wrote that letter to my husband last summer, I have been thinking about my art show. I knew I had to paint, I knew it would be therapeutic, and I also knew, because of Beau's influence, it would be beautiful. Opening Night is approaching with haste! Only twenty-eight days to go! This is a show that I am particularly proud of. I have titled it "Kintsukuroi" which is a Japanese word that translates to "golden repair." Last year while I experienced first-hand what living with a devastated heart feels like, I struggled with how to see myself as whole again. I read a quote that explains,

  `"In Japan, broken objects are often repaired with gold. The flaw is seen as a unique piece of the object's history, which adds to its beauty. Consider this when you feel broken."`
 - UNKNOWN

  This quote was the seed from which this show grew. Each painting is filled with beautiful washes. The colours mix, and meld, and in the moments between the life of the colours, there lies cracks. The cracks are lined or filled with gold. My hope is that anyone who feels broken can look at these works, and see the beauty, and the strength in the repair.
  The show was a success! My heart was so full from the support that my friends, family, and the community showered me with. I even received several commissions for paintings in the Kintsukuroi style for people's nurseries, which truly moved me, and solidified the notion that beauty CAN come from tremendous loss.

"In Japan broken objects are often repaired with gold. The flaw is seen as a unique piece of the object's history, which adds to its beauty. Consider this when you feel broken."

- Unknown

CHAPTER 18
The Mountain

Today I came to a profound realization. Like many of you, I have been on a quest to regain my health, to unearth some answers, to find the right direction, and to head in it. After seeing countless doctors across the country, spending literally thousands of dollars on tests and supplements, and reaching out to anyone who might listen, I finally realized ALL of the answers I have so desperately pined for are all inside of me. I am the only person who knows or who will ever really know, what feels good and what doesn't. My job is not to read any more scientific journals, it is to clean out the external noise, all of the opinions, everything I've read, all of my understanding. This isn't about comprehension, or medical books, or facts. This isn't even about science. It's about energy. It's about getting really quiet and listening. You do know the answers. All of them. You know what fuel your body needs to perform at its best. If you're like me, you've searched for that magic pill or food combination externally. You've exhausted the documentaries available on Netflix, you've seen your fair share of specialists, and read books on books on books. Maybe you've already come to this same conclusion that I have, that children inherently know, that across cultures we can all agree on…That we need to eat as many organic fruits and vegetables as possible, while incorporating clean proteins and whole grains. We need to stay hydrated with the best quality water we have. We need to drink warm clear teas that soothe our tender hearts and aide in our digestion. When we're tired we need to sleep. We need to move our body for no other reason than we can…and how lucky are we that we can! Go to places that grow your energy, that increase your frequency. You already know where these places are. Think about it. Do you feel full after sitting by the lake watching the sunset, or when you're walking through the forest with your dog, or when you're laughing with your very best friends.

These places, these moments in time, these are our therapists, our magic pills. If it is fertility you are worried about stop worrying. Worry is probably one of the biggest obstacles. Start enjoying making love to your partner for no other reason than sheer pleasure. Keep listening. Keep thanking your body for all of the amazing things that it is doing right and keep going, because you can, keep going.

Throughout this year I have continually gone back to Amelia's book *Landon's Legacy*. I think part of the reason why it is so important for people to continue sharing their stories is because for those of us in the early stages of our grief, or whatever it may be that you are going through, if you can find another soul on this planet that has walked down a similar path, if you can connect to their words, and follow their lead, it can make all the difference. Amelia's words became a page in my own survival guide. They also inspired me to tell my story. To layout the path I took in order to climb the mountain in front of me. I think a lot of bereaved parents inherently know why it's important for us all to share our stories, to raise awareness, and to be incredibly raw. For some people it's a matter of life and death. Other women have walked this path and the mountain has swallowed them. I know that death isn't an easy thing to talk about for a lot of people. I also know that stillbirth and child loss can be even more uncomfortable. Having said that, I am all too aware that it is often the MOST therapeutic thing a grieving person can do. We need to talk about our babies because they were real, and they matter. We need to tell our stories, because loss will touch us all, and when we shed light on the darkness it becomes a lot less scary. Light the candles, take part in the movements, listen to the stories, ask questions. We aren't holding on to the past. We are surviving the present and strengthening the foundation of understanding to lift ourselves and others who have fallen upon this difficult journey.

PART VI
Summer

CHAPTER 19
Mother's Day

Summer is here again, and the weather has changed, but instead of enjoying the balmy nights and sun filled days I find myself saddened by the memory of losing Beau in this same weather just a year ago. Thinking back, the entire month of May was hard. Most days even swallowing hurt. As Mother's Day approached, I had some realizations of my own and so I wrote a post that went like this,

I feel naive for not realizing until this year that Mother's Day isn't an easy, joyful, carefree Sunday for a lot of people. If you are holding someone in your heart today because you can't hold them here, you're not alone. We are many. And even though I mostly want to hold down the couch for the next 24hrs, inside, with the curtains drawn, a bigger part of me wants to celebrate what it means to be a woman, the resiliency of the human spirit, the bond between family, the strength of so many women I know, and the power of love. A love that is so strong not even death can touch it. On days like today, let's lean in and feel the love.

My birthday is the day after Mother's Day and Brodie always spoils me, but my favourite gift this year was the Tibetan Prayer Flags that he got me. I remember touching the fabric when I opened them, and dreaming of where they would be hung. I did some reading about the flags and learned that,

"Traditionally, prayer flags are used to promote peace, compassion, strength, and wisdom. The flags do not carry prayers to gods, which is a common misconception; rather, the Tibetans believe the prayers and mantras will be blown by the wind to spread the good will and compassion into all pervading space." - WIKIPEDIA

I also read that you can write the names of people whom you want the prayers to reach directly onto the flags. I didn't yet know where I was going to place the flags, but I knew it had to be somewhere special.

CHAPTER 20
Beau's Birthday

In the days leading up to Beau's birthday, Brodie and I talked about what we wanted to do. We both felt that we didn't want to put too much pressure on ourselves as we knew better than to have any kind of expectation for how the day would go. We both took the day off work, and decided to drive to the Duck Mountains. I had asked around at work for people's favourite places in Manitoba. A few of my colleagues spoke very highly of that area and so we decided we'd hit the road and drive to the pristine lakes they described. Before we left Minnedosa we stopped at Beau's grave. I laid some lilac flowers on his stone, and through our tears we wished him the happiest birthday.

It seemed as though Beau had some surprises for us too, for as we drove we continued to see baby animals coming out of the woods. First, we saw two bear cubs running along the ditch. Then, about an hour later we saw a baby dear running through the forest. Next, in the middle of the road was a tiny chipmunk, and as we turned onto a gravel road to approach the lake a beautiful great-blue-heron took flight directly in front of our windshield, hovering over our vehicle's hood. Brodie had to hit the brakes as to not run into the majestic bird.

We sat by the lake holding Beau in our memories and talking about his curly locks and big hands. We kept driving, and came upon a sign for Baldy Mountain. I had a feeling that Beau's birthday would grow and evolve and organically become the day I felt it should be in my heart but prior to seeing this sign I didn't yet know what that looked like. This sign sparked an idea, that for each of Beau's birthdays we would climb a different mountain. Baldy Mountain is the highest peak in our province. To us it made sense to be in nature, and to be as high as we could be, to feel closer to our son. Yes, we could hop in a plane and that would surely get us higher than Manitoba's tallest summit, but I still wanted my feet on the ground…the same ground that my son's physical body is now a part of. Brodie and I drove to the entrance of the mountain, and got out of the Jeep, as if to attempt the 6km hike right then and there. Unfortunately, the mist was so thick you couldn't see too much, the mosquitos were on a mission, it had started to rain, and we didn't have any proper footwear for the climb. So, we got back in the Jeep and made plans for Beau's next birthday. We decided we would climb a different mountain for each of his birthdays, and we also thought of a place to put the prayer flag. I read a little more about how to properly hang the tapestry and discovered certain days of the year multiply the power of the flags by huge amounts. Beau was born on May 31st and one of the most powerful days to hang the flags is on June 1st. We decided in that very moment, we had a beautiful tradition for our Beau's future birthdays. We would spend his birthday hiking to the top of a different peak, camp overnight breathing in the fresh air, and hang a prayer flag at sunrise the next morning. We drove home both feeling more settled and as the sky darkened we lay by Beau's grave with a candle lit looking for him in the stars. I of course wanted to write something public to wish Beau a happy birthday and this is the message that came out on that day,

And just like that a year has gone by. A year of salty tears, of missing breaths, of sleepless nights, of painful dreams, of rawness, of wonder, of healing, of growth, and of deep deep love. Beau, one year ago today we got to meet you, to hold you and to feel your skin on ours. Today is your birthday and it is the ONLY day I think about EVERY day. In a hundred lifetimes, in a thousand worlds, in every version of reality I would still choose you. You are LOVED, you are MISSED, and like all good things you are wild and free.

CHAPTER 21
A Diagnosis

    Almost exactly a year after losing Beau we got some answers. Beau's complete autopsy came back in that same difficult month of May. The document described his cause of death to be due to several microscopic blood clots in my umbilical cord and placenta. We spent the entire year going over any scenario we could think of, talking to every doctor we could, and no one had any idea of what had happened. I got a phone call from my Rheumatologist in Hamilton who explained that they were now going to diagnose me with a blood clotting disorder called Anti Phospholipid Antibody Syndrome. They explained that it wasn't a 'slam dunk' diagnosis but close enough to make the call. My doctor explained that going forward I needed to be on Heparin injections prior to conception and during the entire pregnancy. I explained that it was possible that I was pregnant already. We started trying again in May, and so it was decided I start the injections immediately just in case.

    My reason for sharing this with you is because autoimmune disorders are rapidly on the rise. In addition to that, a whopping 80% of people with autoimmune diseases are women. Also, if you already have one your chances of developing a second are drastically increased. APS causes the blood to clot, however symptoms may never occur until pregnancy (like in my case). What's maddening is that right now the protocol for administering these inexpensive blood tests, to determine if you have the antibodies associated with the disorder, involves a woman having three or more miscarriages, or a stillborn, yet the intervention can be as simple as taking an Aspirin a day. I am aware that we cannot test for everything during a pregnancy but I am a firm believer that when you know better you do better. Now that I know more I want to try and help other women not go through the same heartache. It is important to advocate for yourself. If you are a woman with an existing autoimmune condition and you plan on starting a family, ask your doctor about being tested for APS. If they dismiss it, kindly ask again. If you get nowhere, get a second opinion. Find a doctor that will run the test.

I waited until my next predicted cycle date in June to take a pregnancy test, and…it was positive. As I write this it is only July, and we are almost ten weeks pregnant with a little peanut growing every day. We've seen the heartbeat and I feel the consistent nausea which I try to remember is a blessing. So, I vow again, to celebrate this baby for every day that I am pregnant, for however long that may be. Brodie and I have very high hopes, but we also know that things can change within a single moment. We know we need to be emotionally strong as we still have a higher chance of having a stillborn, but this bumpy road is ours, and we will honour every day that comes our way.

As the year after Beau has come to an end, I know our grief and our love will continue on. I have learned to do less and be more, to remain open, and to look down. I have learned that control is an illusion, that no amount of suffering will do anyone any good, that I can choose to be happy, that cracks can be beautiful, and that I have been given the gift of inner peace and of true freedom. I thank Beau for this journey, for the transformation, for the lessons, and most of all for choosing me to be his mom.

"In order to be fully alive, we must feel it all....Life isn't meant to be easy, or perfect, or happy all the time. Life is meant to confront us. It will get in our face and push our boundaries and stretch our limits. Life doesn't do this to be cruel. It does this to remind us of our strength and bring us closer to our spirit. In the midst of grieving in a way I've never done before, I feel stronger than I ever have before. It's such a weird paradox. That's the beauty of life. With every twist and tug and pull...With every heartache and break...Life is making us all. Making and molding and polishing our soul – so that we may one day shine even brighter. This is life. I continue to welcome ALL of life – the heartbreak and hope, the pain and the joy, the smiles and the tears. There is room for it all. Above all things, I trust more than ever before that Life is completely and utterly holding me. I don't have to do a thing. Life has got me and if it's not this, it will be something else because that's the way Life works...My heart feels full. Full from love. Full from pain. Full from Life. And that is a beautiful gift." - JULIE SANTIAGO

"I have to believe that my baby will be born alive and healthy"

— Unknown

"I deserve this. It is ok to dream, It is ok to hope. Pregnancy can and will be Beautiful - for as many days as that may be."

— Franchesca Cox

PART VII
Angel Baby Stories

I have dedicated this section of the book to a few of my fellow bereaved mothers. I think that all of our stories are important, and the wisdom, resiliency, courage, and strength that I have seen in these women alone is truly humbling. Thank you for sharing your road, and thank you for helping others find a way to walk through theirs. Many of these women I met at the retreat, some of these women are close friends and some are even family members.

CHAPTER 22
Beckett's story

Name: Gwen Tiggelaar
Angel Baby Name: Beckett Zephaniah Tiggelaar
Most Helpful Resources: Other loss moms who get it and want to share, support and give permission to grieve.
Favourite healing quote: "Grief never ends...But it changes. It's a passage, not a place to stay. Grief is not a sign of weakness, nor a lack of faith. It is the price of love."

The story of Beckett:

On April 20, 2015 I woke up and smiled to myself. I was pregnant with my 4th child (the oldest turned 5 the day before) and I had reached my due date...again. And there were no signs of labour starting soon. I had a prenatal appointment scheduled for that afternoon, and at the last minute grabbed the overnight bag to leave with the kids at the babysitter's house. My last baby was overdue and weighed 11 lb. 1 oz. at birth, so I wondered if I would be encouraged to be induced sooner than later this time around. My appointment started like it had every other time, and then my world came crashing down around me when the doctor was unable to locate my baby's heartbeat. I was sent to the hospital, had an ultrasound which confirmed that he was dead, and then was induced and delivered him that night. Beckett Zephaniah Tiggelaar was born at 10:37 pm, weighing 8 lb. 12 oz. fully and absolutely beautifully formed -

but with a tight knot in his umbilical cord.

I have 9 months worth of memories with Beckett, and 3 years worth of heartache missing and longing for him. The moment we found out that I was pregnant with our 4th child, we started to imagine who this baby would be and how he or she would fit into our busy family. I have memories of excitement (and nervousness) that we shared in the early weeks, when this new life was our special secret. Before we shared our news we had already created a bond with our baby. My pregnancy with Beckett was easy and normal, and he was part of everything I did, growing right below my heart. Those pleasant memories ended suddenly and the piercing pain took over the moment that everything changed. There aren't words to describe the hurt, but it's worth mentioning that I still also remember the swell of pride that I felt when I first laid eyes on our son. We poured over every inch of him and memorized the feel of him in our arms. That beautiful memory will last, and occasionally it will make me smile. But more often I just ache to hold him and feel robbed of the memories we will never get to make.

The last 3 years have been filled with challenges and struggles, marking time since the last time we held our precious son. But we keep putting one foot in front of the other, and the days also include moments filled with excitement, joy, and hope. I read somewhere that grieving isn't the only way to show love for your child, and I hope that Beckett's memory won't live on only because people see our sadness; we are living our lives to reflect that his 40 weeks of life in my womb should be celebrated. He wasn't a "lost pregnancy" or tragic event that should never be spoken about. Beckett was, and is, our beloved son.

CHAPTER 23
Kaiden's Story

Name: Blair
Angel Baby Name: Kaiden
Most Help Resource: Being my own advocate for perinatal loss and mental health.
Quote: "Just when the Caterpillar thought the world was over, it became a butterfly"

Our lives were forever changed on May 19, 2017. My husband and I gave birth to a beautiful baby boy, Kaiden Joel. He was perfect. He looked just like his big sister, Ava. Sadly, Kaiden left us over an hour after being born. Our world has forever been turned upside down.

I had been experiencing severe complications in my pregnancy from 18 weeks until the day we lost Kaiden at 24 weeks. In that time, I was hospitalized for 3 very long weeks, with a 2 year old daughter and a very supportive husband at home. During the time that I was hospitalized I am very grateful to our family who reached out to help us when we needed them the most.

Four days after being released from the hospital our sweet boy was born. Little did we know we would say hello and goodbye within the same day. Shock, sadness, confusion, anger and guilt began to set in that evening. We were confused as to what happened. My husband and I spent the night in the hospital replaying the day's events over and over, wondering what happened and why us?

Over the past year and a half I have met several women who unfortunately share the same sadness as I do. I'm very sad to have met them, however very grateful to have them all in my life now to share our stories of our beautiful babies. I have joined a support group in Regina, SK. It took me a few months to join after we lost Kaiden, however, I am forever grateful I made the decision to go. I have made connections with women & men who have experienced my pain & sadness. The women I have met in this group continue to guide me through some of my darkest days. I've also become a member of the "Twinkle Star Project." A group of women whose mission is to help families who have experienced perinatal loss, just like we have experienced. I chose to do individual counselling in the beginning of my loss journey and I continue to do so from time to time. I feel I have utilized all the resources Saskatchewan has to offer.

I have found healing in talking & sharing my story. I have become my own advocate for perinatal loss. To my husband, Joel & my daughter, Ava thank you from the bottom of my heart. Thank you for being very patient with me in this journey. I love you both so very much and I can't imagine having done this without you both here with me. To my family and friends who continue to guide me through this difficult road I am forever grateful to have each and every one of you in my life. To my fellow bereaved mothers & fathers you are not alone. It is not an easy journey, however you do not have to do it alone. Do not ever feel like there is no one. I too feel your pain. I know what it feels like to be the "elephant" in the room. Do not hesitate to talk. It has truly been my best medicine and has helped me to understand
what has happened, and to process it all-even if I am telling my story over and over again. Let your emotions show. It is okay to cry. It is okay not to cry. My heart is with you all today and always.

Losing Kaiden has forever changed our family. Our daughter, Ava who is now 3 years old knows of her little brother and speaks of him often. Kaiden has taught my husband, Joel, Ava and I to love a little harder. He has given us strength we didn't even know existed within us. Not a day goes by that we don't think about Kaiden or speak his name.

We include Kaiden in all that we do. I am grateful for the time Joel and I got to spend with Kaiden. A memory that I will hold with me for the rest of my life.

On the morning we laid Kaiden to rest a little, blue butterfly landed on my finger while I was having a quiet moment outside with Ava. That little blue butterfly still lingers around our yard to this day. Kaiden, I know you're here with us.

Love to you all.

CHAPTER 24
Marlowe's Story

Name: Bethany
Angel Baby Name: Marlowe

    Hello, my name is Bethany and my husband's name is Andrew and this is the story of our daughter Marlowe.
    Our pregnancy was a surprise. We had been married 4 years and talked about trying to start a family very soon but hadn't actually started trying. We thought it might be difficult to get pregnant because of irregularities with my hormones but I had always prayed that we would get pregnant on our own and that it would be a surprise. So when we found out we were pregnant we were ecstatic!
    I was very blessed with what most would consider a perfect pregnancy. No morning sickness, weird cravings, or crazy mood swings, I didn't have to buy maternity clothes, and our baby grew and developed at the expected rate without any cause for concern. We found out we were having a girl and started decorating her nursery in grey and teal, eagerly anticipating her due date on June 11, 2017.
    I stopped working two weeks beforehand and spent the following week nesting and getting things in order as much as one thinks one can before their first baby arrives. Friday morning started off pretty normal. Andrew and I discussed our list of baby names over coffee and got a couples massage. In the afternoon as I was lying on the couch I thought to

myself I couldn't remember the last time I felt her move. She was extremely active from the very beginning so I became worried. I told Andrew my concerns and we drove to the hospital where they admitted us, brought in the ultrasound machine, and confirmed our worst fears. Our baby girl didn't have a heartbeat.

I was induced and she was born on Saturday June 3, 2017 at 3:08pm. She weighed 6lb 11.4oz and was 20.25 inches long. They discovered when she was born that she had a true knot in her umbilical cord and the cord was wrapped tightly around her neck twice. They ran other tests but in the end the only thing that was wrong was the cord. We named her Marlowe which means "from the hill by the lake" because of where she was conceived.

I thought at first that maybe we would move on from this tragedy and forget this pain but we learned very quickly that moving on isn't really possible, nor is it something we want. Marlowe has become part of our family in every way possible and we are so proud to be her parents. We bring her hat with us when we travel so she can be in our pictures and our family and friends talk about her and remind us that they love her too and that she's just as real to them as she is to us. Her picture hangs on our wall and we think about her every day. Andrew and I are comforted by our belief that Marlowe is in heaven and that we will meet her someday but we still grieve for her and miss the memories that would have been. We pray that someday soon she will have siblings who will be proud to know they have a big sister named Marlowe.

CHAPTER 25
Braden's Story

Name: Meghan and Kristen Jackman
Angel Baby Name: Braden Patrick Jackman
Most Helpful Resources: Landon's Legacy by Amelia Barnes & It's Ok that You're Not Ok by Megan Devine
Favourite Healing Quote: "When there's a fresh wound in your heart, keep it open until it heals. Air it out. Understand it. Dive into it. Be fierce enough to become it. If you ignore it, it won't be able to breathe. If you ignore it, it will merely deepen, spread, and resurface later, wanting to release. And when later happens, it will hurt even more, because when later happens, you won't know what you're bleeding for. Remain with it until it clears, and watch the beauty pour into your openness. Remain open to feel lightness. Remain open to feel free."- Victoria Erickson

<u>AND I HELD HER HAND</u>
Trying to grow our family is exciting,
Until it doesn't work
Months turn to years
She sits crying on the cold bathroom tile
Helpless, I sit beside her, and I hold her hand

After the attempts, the waiting, the blood tests,
Scans, shots, meetings, "next times", and loss,
It works

We celebrate every symptom, dancing in the kitchen
This is all beautifully real and I hold her hand

We tell our parents they are to be grandparents
We piece together a gentle nursery, with my Gram's rocking chair and homemade blankets,
She glows in the daytime and laughs in her sleep
As we sing to him, I feel my first kick
We fall in love with our sweet, wild boy and I hold her hand

I watch her on the dance floor, rolling to Proud Mary
Out of breath and laughing, she holds her large belly
Beautifully happy, she is lit up from within
Later, we dance slowly, our wiggly boy joins along
The three of us move together and I hold her hand

We pick out the perfect tree
It is her favorite day of the year
As we decorate, she stops to let me feel his strong kicks
I give her belly raspberries and he responds with his dancing hands and feet
He is almost here and I hold her hand

In an instant I lose them both
Our sweet, wild boy is gone,
And so is the life in her eyes
Darkness moves in and she turns to gray, shaking stone
I fall to my knees and I hold her hand

Six pounds, two ounces, nineteen inches,
Sandy brown hair, and her face
Joy and a sinking ache
The three of us share a hospital bed until we run out of time
Trembling, she screams as he is taken away, and I hold her hand

She clutches his hat as she is wheeled down the hallway
Our boy is cold and left behind
She is stitched and empty
Wailing in the shower as her milk comes in
Drowning, drenched with pain and I hold her hand

I find myself reaching for her belly, only to remember
It hits, sick and gasping for air
She catches me and her full eyes lower
Baby spoons with the silverware and bottles in the cabinet
Heaviness hits my throat and I hold her hand

In six months-time, we build a garden
To have something to tend to, to nurture
We find joy in watching it grow
We are broken but trying
His light pours out of our darkness and I hold her hand

CHAPTER 26
Daniel's Story

Name: Felicia Blackburn
Angel Baby Name: Daniel

Having a child was something that never came naturally to me. I was never one of those women who "just knew" they wanted to be a mom. My husband on the other hand, always knew he wanted children and the more the better.
When my husband and I got married in 2009, we decided we would wait a few years and then let God decide our journey to parenthood. This is the hardest part for me to accept. I never planned my pregnancies, I never tracked my cycle or did IVF or did any of those things people do to make a baby (note there is nothing wrong with doing any of these things, they just weren't for me). We let nature take its course. Yet here I am - 33 years old, three pregnancies and no babies in my arms.

I never had any trouble getting pregnant. My first and second pregnancies happened within a few months of not using birth control. Both pregnancies ended at 8 and 9 weeks, diagnosed as "missed miscarriages". Do you know what a missed miscarriage is? Neither did I. A missed miscarriage is where your baby just dies and you continue to have symptoms of pregnancy. How cruel is that? You are walking around thinking you are carrying a healthy baby within you all the while, the baby has no heartbeat and you are none the wiser. I gave birth to my first two babies at home in the bathroom. I didn't look at them, I didn't hold them, I just flushed them down the toilet. There were no funerals, no recognition of their short lives. Just as quickly as they were here, they were gone.

I know what you are thinking -how can she talk about these miscarriages in such a casual, heartless fashion? Trust me, at the time it felt like the end of the world. It's not that I didn't care about those babies or didn't want those pregnancies; I know I am blessed to be able to get pregnant. I know there are thousands of women out there who cannot get pregnant and for that I am truly grateful. It is a combination of factors that I have only recently come to realize that makes me able to talk about them so directly.
With the first pregnancy, I had a lot of guilt about the miscarriage. Since I wasn't sure that I wanted children it was MY FAULT the baby had died. With the second pregnancy, I was so scared about having a miscarriage again that I didn't even bond with the baby or truly accept that I was pregnant until it was too late. I will always love those babies and wonder who they would have been. What I have learned since is that God was protecting my heart. He was preparing me and making me stronger so that I could survive what was coming.

After my first two miscarriages, I was extremely fearful of trying for another pregnancy. In fact, we continued to use condoms as birth control for several years. About 2 1/2 years after my second miscarriage, I was ready to try again and see what God had in store for us.

In early 2016 I found out I was pregnant with baby number three. This had to be it – third time is the charm, right? The pregnancy had been going well. I was feeling great, the baby had a heartbeat and was
growing and we had made it passed the "safe zone". Things were looking good. Fast forward, to my 20 week ultrasound.
My life changed forever that day. Seven words from the doctor's mouth turned my life upside down. "There's

something wrong with the baby's heart". Fear, sadness, speculation, guilt, blame. So many emotions. So much disbelief.

Our baby was diagnosed a week later with a severe congenital heart defect called Hypo-plastic Left Heart Syndrome. This basically meant our baby would be born with only half a heart. After meeting with a pediatric heart specialist we were provided with three options: 1) terminate the pregnancy 2) three-step heart surgery or 3) heart transplant.
Why was this happening to us? After so much loss couldn't we just catch a break?

While none of the options given were ideal, we chose to proceed with the heart surgery and leave the rest up to God. We were told that if our baby had the surgery they would lead a relatively normal life but would just have a few more doctors' visits than most kids. Chances of surviving the first surgery were 90%. We also found out we were having a boy. Things were looking up.

My pregnancy continued uneventful. The baby was developing normally and his broken heart kept beating.
I don't remember the first time I felt a real kick from the baby. It took a while for me to distinguish kicks from gas. When the movement was clear, the more kicks I felt, the closer I felt to him. What an amazing thing to feel your child from the inside. After everything we had gone through, a part of me and my husband was living and thriving inside me and it is truly a miracle. I remember staring at my stomach and touching it constantly with fascination and so much love. There was really a baby in there!

At 42 weeks, my labour was induced after failing to progress on my own. After 17 hours, the baby's heartbeat suddenly dropped and he was delivered via emergency C-section. After this long journey of loss and pain, our son was finally here. We named him Daniel Gabriel. He was so beautiful. He had my nose and mouth and his dad's eyes and forehead.
After checking Daniel's heart and considering the other factors of his traumatic birth, we were told he was no longer

a candidate for the surgery, nor could he receive a heart transplant. Our only option was to make him as comfortable as possible and wait for him to pass away. 33 hours after his birth, Daniel took his last breath in my arms surrounded by family.

I immediately noticed how empty I felt. There were no more kicks. When I rubbed my belly now there was nothing but a hallow shell of what used to hold my entire world. Instead of taking home a newborn baby, I left with empty arms. Instead of planning feedings and newborn pictures, I was making funeral arrangements. It's amazing how much can change in such a short time.

If you are still reading this, you likely now understand why I feel the way I do about my miscarriages. I loved those babies as I love Daniel but their purpose was never clear to me. Now I know, had I not experienced those miscarriages and strengthened and grown as a person, there is no way I would be here today. The pain of losing a child, no matter at what stage, changes you significantly. It takes everything from you. It makes you hurt so badly you don't know how you can make it another day. You feel sad all the time. You feel sad even when you experience joy. You feel guilty for living. You cry more and you reflect on life. You struggle with finding purpose and you are desperate to make sure your child is remembered.

In the midst of all this pain and heartache, there is good change. You love people more. You appreciate your surroundings. You stop to smell the roses. You read "one more story" to your niece. You give your husband a kiss and hug every time you see him. You talk to your dad on the phone for as long as he wants. You appreciate life.
I wouldn't trade the short time we had with Daniel for anything in the world. His life is linked to mine forever. His death changed me as a person but does not define me. I will miss him every day of my life but I will move forward and make him proud. Daniel chose me to be his mom and I will be forever grateful.

CHAPTER 27
Noah's Story

Name: Amber
Angel Baby Name: Noah
Most Helpful Resource: Kelly + Tony (parents)
Favourite Healing Quote: "If love could have saved you, you would have lived forever."

For as long as I can remember, my answer to the question "What do you want to be when you grow up?" has always been "A mother." Something I assumed would come naturally and easily when the time was right. Unfortunately, the universe had other plans. I was diagnosed with Endometriosis at age 15 and while I was advised of the effects it may have on future fertility, I followed all recommendations to lower the chances of further reproductive damage. I was put on hormonal birth control pills and had a laparoscopic procedure done to remove any lesions. At age 26 I was in a committed, serious relationship where the excitement of having children came up frequently. We both agreed we were ready to start actively trying to conceive in late December of 2016. Initially I was ecstatic, after all this was all I had ever wanted and my partner and I had such immense love for one another, though I quickly started having second thoughts. We had another conversation and decided to wait. Over the course of the next few weeks strange occurrences and conversations with friends and family kept happening that seemed as though the universe was trying to tell me something. By now it was the first week of February and I hadn't missed a period, but after an entire carton of eggs turned out to be double yolks (an old wives tale of pregnancy) I decided to humour myself and find out for sure. On Monday, February 6th, 2017 I picked up a test, took a deep breath and headed to the bathroom. I remember those two pink lines appearing before I could even stand up. How did this happen? I was still on the pill and my cycle was seemingly regular. I simultaneously felt scared shitless and full of excitement. My partner was over the moon entirely, but something inside me was fuelling my concerns. We sat there for a while trying to figure out how far along I could possibly be since I just had what I assumed was my period a few weeks prior. Soon enough we'd find out that's not quite what that was. Three days later I woke up to blood - a lot of blood. We called my OB-Gyn immediately and they informed us there was a high chance I was miscarrying. I felt immense guilt, I felt as though somehow my inner hesitations willed this to happen. They told us to monitor the amount of blood I was losing and to come in for blood work the following day and again 48 hours later to compare HCG levels. I was scheduled a follow up for the following Tuesday. The Dr. said my HCG levels were still increasing but not doubling and we needed to do an ultrasound. I remember watching the technicians face as she scanned my abdomen, it seemed to be entirely expressionless until all of a sudden she stopped, and there it was - a sort of sadness and disappointment had taken over her. She quickly ended the session and told me the Dr. would be with me shortly. I don't remember much about the rest of that appointment, as soon as the Dr. came in and told me the pregnancy was ectopic and "not viable" every other word seemed muffled. My HCG levels were just within the guidelines to qualify for Methotrexate and I was administered the shot a few minutes later. The physical side effects I experienced from the medicine were minimal but emotionally I was destroyed. I felt as though I was being forced into having an abortion. I was made aware how detrimental an ectopic pregnancy would be to the mother's body if left untreated but it didn't change the fact that I was ending a life inside of me. That is when my relationship started to crumble. I went into a deep depression and shut down entirely. I didn't want to talk, I didn't want to be touched and I certainly didn't want to look at the man whom I felt like I let down. Two weeks later I started experiencing severe cramping and wound up at the Emergency Room. More blood work verified my HCG levels were still rising and the fetus was still growing - the Methotrexate didn't work. In an attempt to save my left Fallopian Tube I was administered a second dose of Methotrexate rather than going in for surgery. Around this time my partner and I separated and he moved out. The toll the loss of pregnancy had taken on our relationship was astounding. I continued to have cramping for the next few weeks so my OB-Gyn wanted to see me. They did another ultrasound to confirm the pregnancy was terminated and found just the opposite - the two rounds of Methotrexate had not worked and my left tube was starting to rupture. I was immediately taken to the Hospital and prepped for surgery. The next few weeks are sort of hazy, I remember being told after waking up from surgery that my Fallopian Tube had irreparable damage and had to be removed entirely. She mentioned that it was likely the prior damage to my tubes caused from Endometrial scarring that caused the fertilized egg to get stuck. She told me I was somewhere between 12 and 16 weeks along by the time the fetus was removed and that I was "incredibly lucky" to have made it that far without a total rupture of my tube and severe internal bleeding. I don't know that I'd call that "lucky". I went to stay with my folks a few hours away for the following week to heal. My depression intensified and so did my anger. I was mad at myself, angry at passing pregnant women I encountered, furious at some women in my life that I felt didn't "deserve" the children they were blessed with. Most of all I was upset with my body and its inability to give me the one thing I wanted most in the world - a child. I spent the next few months drinking heavily, hardly sleeping and barely nourishing myself in an attempt to somehow punish my body for the heartache it caused me. After putting so much time and energy into being angry with myself I finally accepted the truth, that sometimes shit just happens. This wasn't some sort of karmic payback, or the universe punishing me. Bad things happen to people every single day and I had to make a conscious effort to not allow this negative experience to dictate how I would approach life or feel about myself. I do think I have a lot of healing left to do and I am very much terrified of the day I decide to try to conceive again, but I am so thankful I was able to eventually release the loss of that baby with love. Some days the hurt is still very much present and deafening, other days it's a loving and humbling presence in my heart. All I know is this loss taught me how incredibly and deeply the human heart can feel and I will be forever thankful for that.

Brodie and I on our wedding day

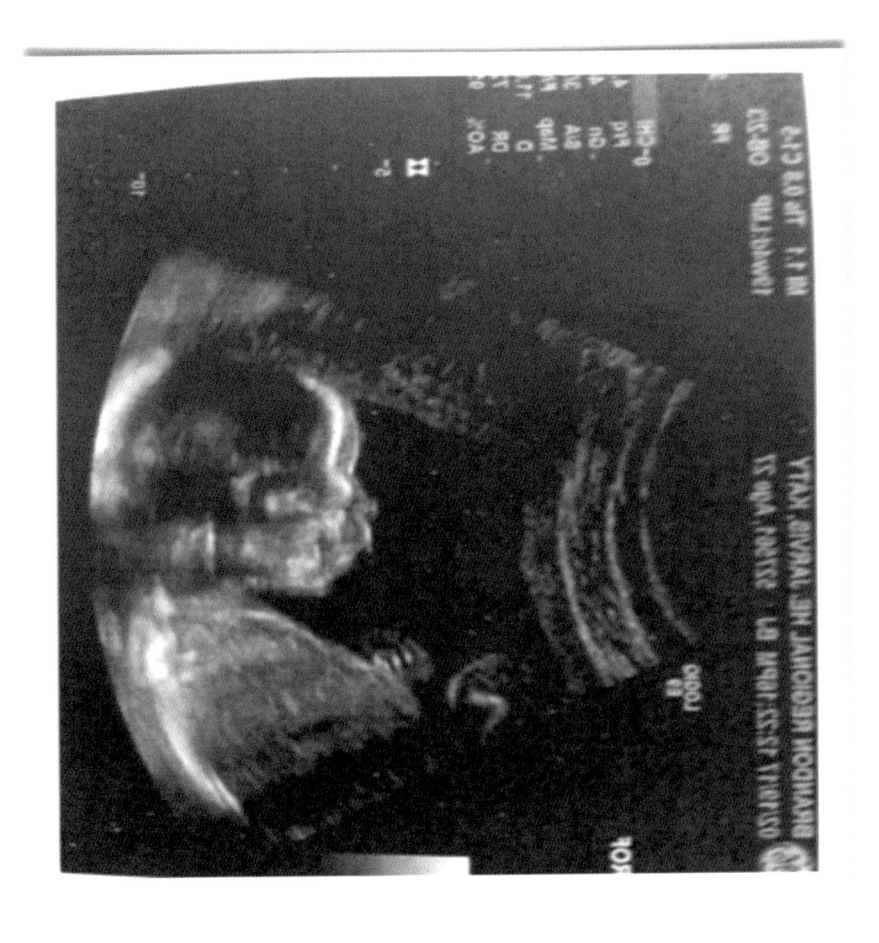

Beau at our 20 week ultrasound

Me, eight months pregnant with Beau

The photo we used to announce Beau's departure

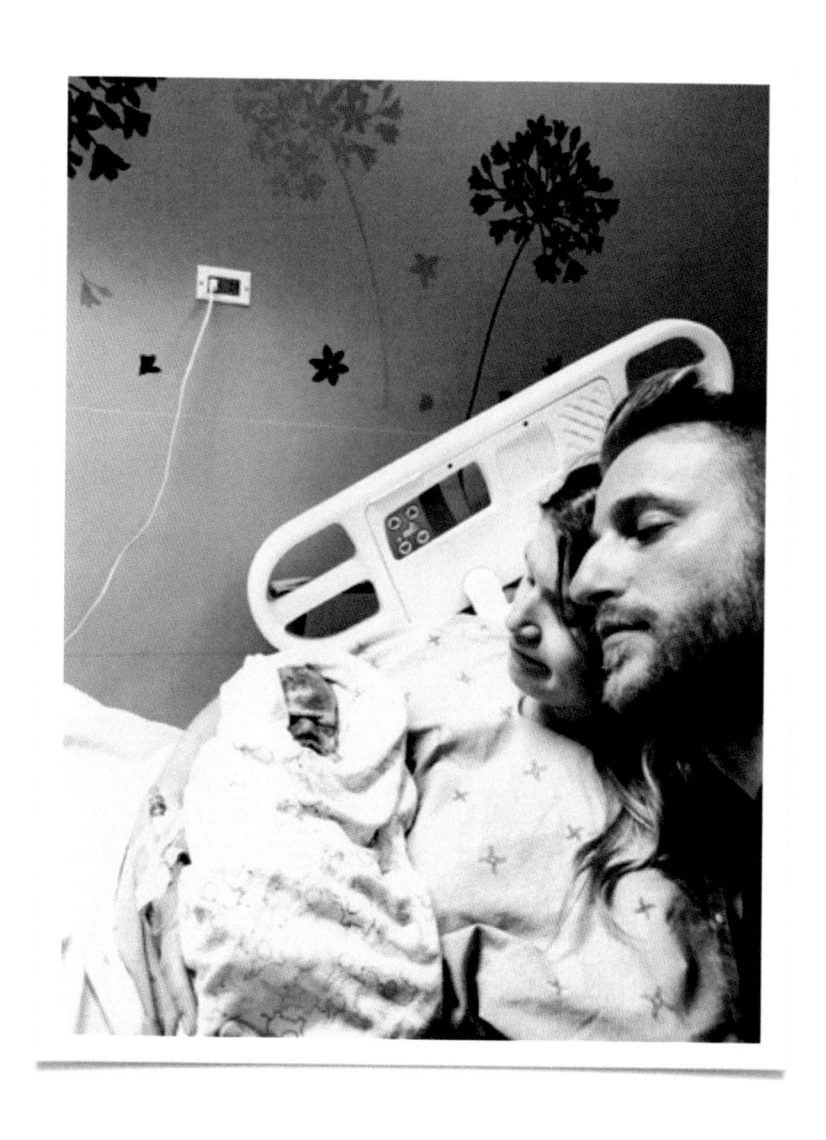

Brodie and I with Beau after delivery

Our Keepsake Shadow Box

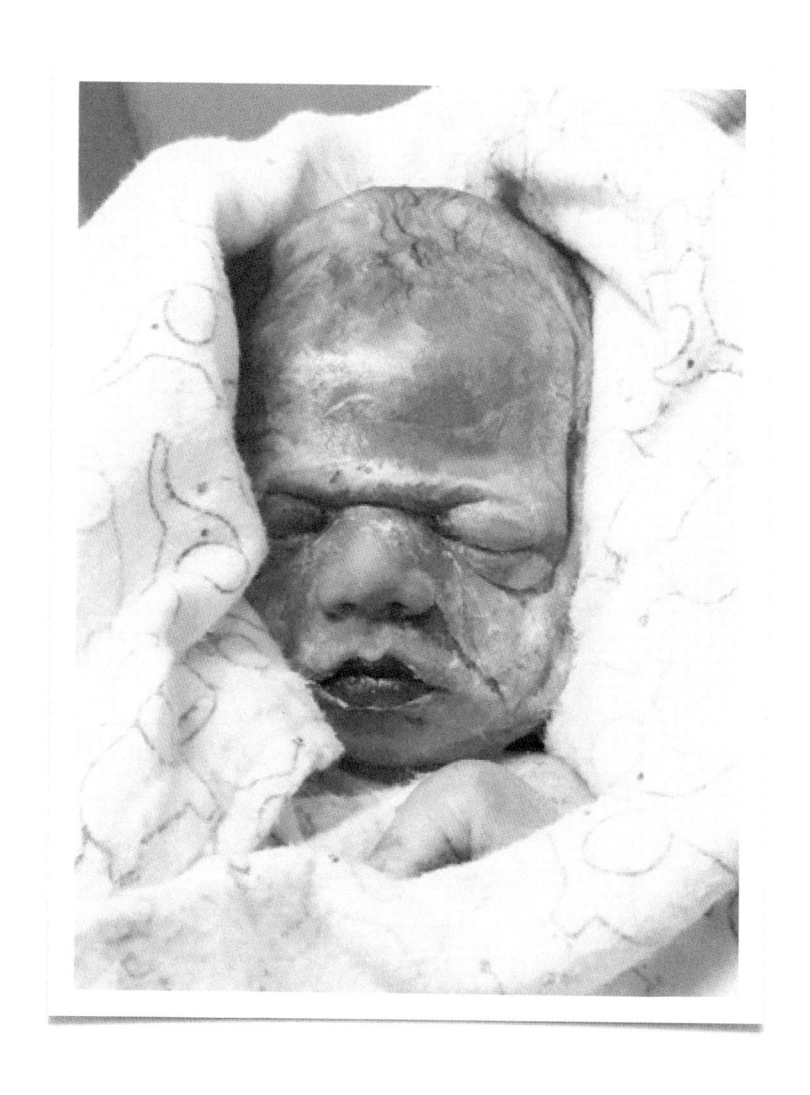

Our Beautiful Boy

Beau's resting place and stone

Landon's Legacy Retreat

My Tribe of Loss Mama's at Landon's Legacy Retreat

Beau's Star

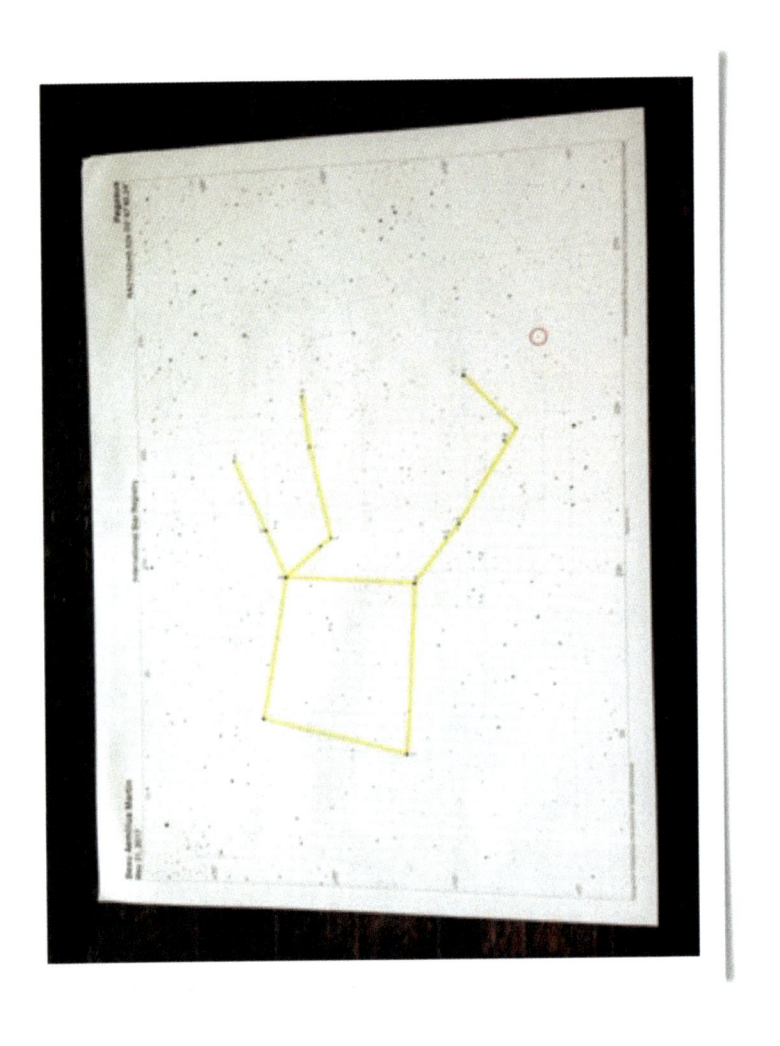

A parking spot on Pegasus

The first Beau Bears

The first Beau Bears

Pregnancy and Infant Loss Awareness, Wave of Light Movement

Getting ready for the art show!

Opening night!

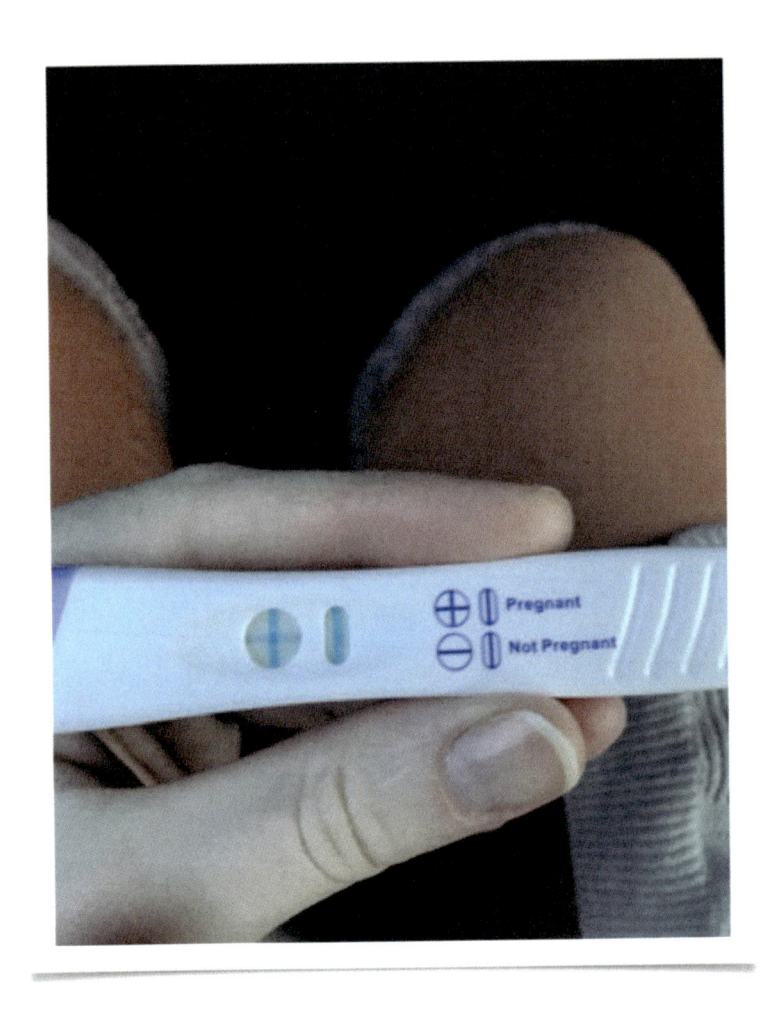

Pregnancy number three, and a hope filled heart!

Waiting on our baby girl to arrive!

THE AUTHOR

Katy was born in 1989, and grew up in the small town of Magnetawan, Ontario. Her parents are Peter and Carmen Jarvis and she has an older brother named Dylan. Katy currently resides with her loving husband Brodie, personality filled dog Piper, and rainbow baby Rori, in Minnedosa, Manitoba. She teaches Art at the high school in Neepawa and continues to be a practicing artist herself. You can follow her work, her writing and teaching career at:

www.theyearafter-katyemartin.com
www.katyscanvas.com

Or

Contact Katy at
katyeileenmartin@gmail.com
Facebook: The Year After
Instagram @katyscanvas

Made in the USA
Lexington, KY
23 November 2019